THE BEAUTIFUL LIE
Finding Faith in a World Gone Mad

Tobin Crenshaw

Copyright © 2018 Tobin Crenshaw

All rights reserved. No part of this book may be used or reproduced in any manner whatsoever without prior written consent of the authors, except as provided by the United States of America copyright law.

Published by Best Seller Publishing®, Pasadena, CA
Best Seller Publishing® is a registered trademark
Printed in the United States of America.

ISBN 978-1-949535-36-5

This publication is designed to provide accurate and authoritative information with regard to the subject matter covered. It is sold with the understanding that the publisher is not engaged in rendering legal, accounting, or other professional advice. If legal advice or other expert assistance is required, the services of a competent professional should be sought. The opinions expressed by the authors in this book are not endorsed by Best Seller Publishing® and are the sole responsibility of the author rendering the opinion.

Most Best Seller Publishing® titles are available at special quantity discounts for bulk purchases for sales promotions, premiums, fundraising, and educational use. Special versions or book excerpts can also be created to fit specific needs.

For more information, please write:
Best Seller Publishing®
1346 Walnut Street, #205
Pasadena, CA 91106
or call 1(626) 765 9750
Toll Free: 1(844) 850-3500
Visit us online at: www.BestSellerPublishing.org

Unless otherwise noted, all scripture quotations are taken from the Holy Bible, New International Version. Copyright 1973, 1978, 1984 International Bible Society. Used by permission of Zondervan. All rights reserved.

Scripture taken from The Source or (TSNT) Copyright © 2004 by Ann Nyland. Used by permission of Smith and Stirling Publishers. All rights reserved.

Website: www.tobincrenshaw.com

Contents

Chapter 1. A New Direction 1

Chapter 2. When All Things Become Possible 37

Chapter 3. Decisions Make the Difference 59

Chapter 4. Breakthrough Living 73

Chapter 5. Something to Believe In 95

Chapter 6. Grace Is Greater 115

Chapter 7. When Faith Becomes Sight 141

Chapter 8. A Remarkable New Identity 159

Chapter 9. Beyond Belief 171

Chapter 10. A New Life 181

beautiful lie (byoōodəfəl lī): a false belief that is closely held due to a convincing presentation

CHAPTER 1

A NEW DIRECTION

"You know right from wrong. You just don't care. And that's the most natural thing in the world."[1]

– **Don Falcone** (Roy Scheider), *Romeo Is Bleeding* (1993)

When Nelson Mandela was released from prison and became the leader of South Africa, he established panels to investigate acts of brutality that had taken place under apartheid. One particular case purportedly involved a woman who was forced to watch her husband be killed by lawless police officers. Unconscionably, the men had also killed her son several years prior. Before her husband drew his final breath, he whispered to her, "Forgive them."

Several years had come and gone since the men had committed these atrocities, and now finally, her torturers had been brought to trial. The woman was asked to be present for the sentencing of the men, and the judge asked her what she felt would be a fitting punishment.

Nigerian minister D. K. Olukoya notes that the courtroom quietly waited as the former mother and wife gave her response, saying, "I want three things."[2] Gazing at the lead officer, she continued, "I want him to take me to the place where they burned my husband's body. I would like to gather up the dust and give him a decent burial."[3]

Second, the woman shared that she had a lot of love left in her heart to give and requested the officer be required to meet with her twice a month so she could be a mother to him.

"Third, I would like this man to know that he is forgiven by God, and that I forgive him, too. And, I would like someone to come and lead me by the hand to where he is so I can embrace him and he can know my forgiveness is real."[4] At that moment, the officer fainted. The courtroom sat in silence until someone began to sing "Amazing Grace." Others joined in the song, filling the entire courtroom with the words of the penetrating hymn.

In a similar vein, Marguerite Barankitse suffered tremendous loss in Burundi, East Africa, during the murderous conflict between the Tutsi and Hutu people. Though she survived, several of her family members were slaughtered before her eyes. In response to such horror, she opened an orphanage where children from both the Tutsi and Hutu are embraced. She eventually forgave the murderer who burned her three aunts alive, even visiting him in prison. She shares that today, *love* is her vocation.[5]

Or consider an Assam family in late nineteenth century India. Baptized during the Welsh revival, they were soon sentenced to die, as such a public declaration of a foreign faith in Hindu dominated India was considered traitorous. Given time to consider renouncing their decision or facing execution, the husband and father replied, "I have decided to follow Jesus, and there is no turning back." The persecutors then took and killed his two children. The man responded, "The world can be behind me, but the cross is still before me." The men grabbed his wife, demanding one last time they renounce the gospel or die. The husband responded, "Though no one is here to go with me, still I will follow Jesus." At that, the mob killed them both.

Gazing upon the atrocities they committed, guilt began to spread over the killers. Sometime later, revival reached the village and the family's' murderers begged for forgiveness. With broken hearts, they became trophies of God's grace. The words of the family were preserved by evangelist Sandhu Sundar Singh, who later turned them into the much-loved hymn.[6]

Where does mercy and strength like that come from? Can one person really make a difference? Is it possible in this crazy, mixed-up world to have a passionate marriage, a thriving faith, dreams worth achieving, and true fulfilment?

Though we may not know each other personally, I believe you and I want the same thing: *a life worth living*! We want a life filled with excitement, a faith that is solid enough to match the breakneck speed at which we live, and inspiration and motivation to daily move towards goals that are the ultimate expression of who we are at our core.

There is a way to live an uncommon life, but it will take doing some things we have never done and unlearning some things we may have believed for years. It will mean going deeper so we can go further.

It has been said that there are two possibilities in life: either God exists, or he does not, and both possibilities are frightening. On the one hand, we take comfort in believing there are answers to life's biggest questions; on the other, we wonder if the truth can ever be known.

In a given year, some 20,000 men and women leave pastoral positions never to return again; most are disillusioned with the selfishness they encounter in people who claim to know better. A few years ago, fed up with the unethical behavior of certain manipulative leaders, I made that number 20,001. I then spent many years working in the criminal justice field, my job carrying me from prisons to courtrooms.

It was during this time I met an inmate named Shannon. He was a model prisoner, and I was part of the exit program he was required to pass through to gain his freedom. He had already spent years in prison as a low-level heroin dealer, and now, after months of good behavior, he was eligible for an early release.

I served as his probation officer and mentor as he transitioned from prison to a halfway house, and eventually to home. He had to pass 6 months of life skill and relationship classes that I was teaching, stay drug-free, and find someone willing to give him a job.

During class, he quickly distinguished himself as someone who was both intelligent and funny. Within the first week, he started regularly sharing jokes. It would often be the highlight of the hour, bringing smiles to even the hardest criminal faces. Before long, the other inmates began to come to class anticipating a chance to hear a good joke and to share laughter in a place mostly void of joy.

Other instructors would stop me in the hall after hearing laughter coming from the classroom and ask what I was teaching. I would just smile and tell them it was Shannon entertaining the group. In the end, he graduated from the program early. He not only found employment and remained drug free, he also signed up to take college courses.

I saw Shannon one last time on the street; he thanked me for believing in him and for helping him stay on track and out of trouble. I told him I was proud of what he had accomplished; he was poised to accomplish great things.

Fast-forward less than a year. Four teens, two girls and two boys were found executed in a basement. They had been lined up, forced on their knees, and shot in the back of the head. It was a quadruple homicide that shocked the community. What happened the next day forever changed the way I viewed people and simple answers.

Shannon and an accomplice were the murderers—cold-blooded killers, flaunting what they had done, remorseless. Before their arrests, they took time to post pictures of themselves on social media. They took photos of their smiling faces, posing with the wads of cash they had made from drug sales just hours after they had murdered four people.

This and other similar events have led me to seek to more fully understand human nature. I wanted to grasp the dynamics of authentic personal change, and the reality of what it would really take for a person to turn their life around, whether it was a couple on the edge of divorce, a person contemplating suicide, someone who simply wanted to reach a long-term goal, or one of the many depressed people I have worked with finally finding peace of mind.

Through this process, I completed graduate studies, taught psychology at the university level, and became a certified strategic interventionist when I completed my coach training at Robbins-Madanes Training under my teachers Tony Robbins, Cloe Madanes, Mark Peysha, and Magali Peysha. I was also able to travel the world to learn from wise spiritual teachers, to consult with and counsel numerous individuals and groups, and to read several hundred books on the power of faith and the forces of personal growth.

After five years of working in the criminal justice system, I did something mostly unheard of: I returned to ministry. Only this time, I came with a deeper faith and solid answers to the problems that haunt individuals. I have long since discarded naïve beliefs and platitudes. Much of this book will be sharing the lessons, tools, and strategies I uncovered that you can use to experience a dynamic faith, lasting fulfillment, and sustainable emotional, relational and spiritual health.

In the Marine Corps, I was a military policeman, serving in a variety of places, from Washington D.C. to Okinawa, Japan. Some of the worst calls were domestic violence dispatches. In the United States, a woman is battered every 15 seconds by her husband or boyfriend; four of these women die each day.[7] What some men will do to women is unbelievable. My partner would regularly shake his head and ask night after night, "What is wrong with people?"

What *is* wrong with people? It seems that confusion and division have become the new norm. But there are men and women of high character in the world, as well as down through history, who, like the men and women at the beginning of the chapter, make what are seemingly miraculous choices. These champions beckon us to raise our standards, to live differently, and to know that what can seem so impossible can become possible. As China's Wang Qishan wisely shares, "Unattainable goals appeal to heroes."[8]

In the first century, the Apostle Paul challenged people to live above being "mere men"[9] who were only interested in themselves. He knew from experience that people could be far greater than they could conceive, yet many had settled for their lesser selves.

There is a story in the life of Napoléon, the French Emperor, in which he is at a parade when his horse starts to rear after being startled. While other men froze, a young enlisted soldier rushed in and grabbed the reigns, calming the animal. Napoléon looked at the man and said, "Thank you, *Captain*." In a moment of promotion, he was given an entirely new identity, elevated beyond whom he previously saw himself to be. As we will see, the same can be true for each one of us as we refuse to let our past or history define us.

So the story went something like this: Banks must lend money to make a profit. Companies began to lend to one another at a lower interest rate, so the banks lost business. So, banks turned to car loans. But car companies began to make loans to customers. Before long, banks lost car loans *and* corporate loans. So, the banks turned to home loans (at times, even charging 18% interest).

People couldn't afford the loans so: 1) the banks lowered their standards to qualify (it was a no-lose situation because they knew the citizens would bail them out of any foreclosures), 2) they loaned money to other countries (you could make $50 million in a single swoop with one loan to a company overseas versus trying to find millions of American customers). To top it all off, loan officers got bonuses for the *quantity* of loans.

Construction companies were given great interest rates to make up for the home loans the banks lost. With such tempting interest rates for their businesses, contractors took the loans and began to build houses—*lots* of houses. Before long, supply outgrew demand and the economy suffered a huge housing crash. Banks found themselves in desperate trouble when the contractors and mortgage owners couldn't pay their bills. The result was financial ruin for many families.

Sound familiar? It is, only the year was not 2008—the year of the Great Recession many individuals and countries are still recovering from; it was the Savings and Loan crisis of the 1980s.[10] As Paul Harvey once said, "When there are times like these, we need to remember there have always been times like these."

Today, people are sharply divided by political parties and ideological beliefs, becoming more and more convinced that those on the other side of the fence (as they define it) are not just wrong, but they are to be maligned or ignored. Trust in the government is at an all-time low. Private conversations of elected officials are now public fodder on social media, and rarely a week goes by without the seedy secrets of some politician coming to light. Again and again people dream of finally electing men and women who will do the honorable thing and bring about positive reformation. In truth, history is littered with the painful results of trusting men in power, hoping they will be able to control their desire to rule over others or to sell their integrity to the highest bidder.

At a seminar, I listened to a fascinating study where teams travelled to different countries to try a simple experiment. Two strangers were randomly chosen and told they were to divide a hundred dollars. They would draw straws to determine who was player one, and who was player two.

The rules were simple: player one had a single chance to divide the money any way they chose. Player two could agree to the offer, and they both would walk away with money, or player two could reject the offer, and neither got paid.

Most people ended up splitting the money 50/50. A few ended up dividing the money 60/40 when player one's greed got the best of them. However, an interesting phenomena happened when player one tried to split the money 70/30. All around the world, the results were the same: player two refused anything above the 60/40 split.

Remember, rejection of player one's offer meant that both parties were left empty handed. Had they been presented $30 from the start and knew nothing about what the second party would get, they would have been happy. But when they saw someone getting more than they would, they became upset. "You mean he gets $70, and I *only* get $30? No deal!"

When questioned why they would not accept walking away with $30, the players responded, "I would rather have nothing before I would allow the other person to receive that much more money than me." Rather than take free money, it became more important to punish someone they felt was taking advantage of them. When we focus only on self, we lose in the end.

Leaders of all stripes continue to affirm the well-known truth about absolute power. Many seek promotions only to dominate others in an attempt to alleviate the pain of their own struggles with low self-esteem and unresolved inner child issues.

Financial organizations have too often shown they care only for the almighty dollar. Citigroup was recently fined $425 million dollars for manipulating interest rates. Wells Fargo was caught opening hundreds of thousands of credit cards without permission from their customers.[11] Years ago, President Andrew Jackson, fed up with crooked financial institutes and banks whose greed created another depression in the early nineteenth century railed, "You are a den of thieves and vipers and I intend to rout you out. If the people understood the rank injustices of our money and banking system, there would be a revolution by morning."[12]

A few years ago, I owned a home in southern Ohio. One day, we noticed a crack in the wall of our garage. It was sizable and had evidently gone unnoticed for some time as it started from the ground and had travelled several feet up the wall. We immediately called our insurance company who quickly dispatched an agent. He stayed less than five minutes, snapped a few pictures, and drove away.

Three days letter, we received a notice by registered mail. The message was simple: our insurance company was dropping our coverage because the damage to our garage wall was deemed extensive and dangerous, and the crack was due to an *earthquake*, something this particular insurance company conveniently did not cover.

I have lived in Ohio for most of my life; we do not have earthquakes that cause damage, and the idea that an insurance agent could come to such a conclusion in a matter of seconds is simply ludicrous. What do you do when a company you pay so you can receive peace of mind refuses to do their job and lies so they can make a profit at your expense? The wisest man who ever lived warned, "Whoever loves money never has enough; whoever loves wealth is never satisfied with their income."[13] Over and over we witness companies trading integrity to line their own pockets. You would think we would have learned by now. As another wise man wrote, "Cursed is the one who trusts in man."[14]

High-profile media members have been caught in scandal after scandal. Drug overdoses, affairs, suicides, abuses of power and even murder have become commonplace. On screen, Hollywood continues to push some of the most vulgar material men have ever conceived, all with an agenda to reshape culture in their own image.

Eighty years ago, Robert Johnson claimed the devil taught him how to play the guitar at the famous crossroad he would sing about. An addict and serial adulterer, his first two wives died, the last one after suffering a nervous breakdown. He would often talk about selling his soul to the devil, and it is said on the day he died he had gone mad. His life ended at 27 when he was poisoned by an angry husband. *Johnson is considered the father of modern rock and roll.* It would seem little has changed in the entertainment industry.[15]

Faith in the medical community is failing as people are tired of simply being given one more prescription to drug them into oblivion without solving much of anything. Doctors provide legal narcotics, which have proven more addictive than street drugs, leaving people dependent upon more and more pills just to function day to day.

As Ty Bollinger notes, "Typically, when you meet someone who is taking multiple prescription drugs, they are mentally fuzzy, sickly in appearance, chronically fatigued, and emotionally unstable and depressed. If you head down to your local organic market and approach the healthiest people you find, why don't you ask which prescription drugs are responsible for their health? After looking a bit dazed and confused, they will likely tell you they do not take prescription drugs!"[16] Just like Hippocrates said sixteen centuries ago, "The natural healing force within us is the greatest force in getting well."

Religious institutions have housed and hidden dark secrets and unsavory leaders, from thieves to pedophiles. I myself have had to fire abusive musicians from churches. I've also encountered and had to remove too many greedy, dishonest assistant pastors and chairmen who were complete moral failures and wanted nothing other than to get their hands on a congregation's money. In each case, these men failed to heed wise counsel. As Solomon warned centuries ago, you cannot correct a fool.[17]

One particular pastor I confronted about plagiarism and anger issues refused to correct his path. The church that employed him continued to support this man after I left, believing he would change. A few months later, they arrived for services on

Sunday morning to find the minister had taped a note to the front door that explained that overnight, he had secretly cleaned out the parsonage and left town for a better-paying position in another state.

Then there was the choir director who worked on the city council. One day, he announced he was leaving his wife and kids, and he did, *for another man*. I could share story after story of such moral failures just in people I have known, let alone the more prominent scandals that have been covered by the media.

It is widely accepted that there is a vast difference between a justice system and a legal system. The latter is what we have; the former is what we wish was true. From politicians to judges to religious leaders and managers of financial institutes, it seems the further we go along in history, the more people move away from true north.

Yet amidst all this, there is an answer, one closer than you can even imagine. But it will take effort on our part. It will take becoming better. It will mean moving from belief to action, and committing to unlearning much of what we have been programmed to believe.

It has been well said that a deeper spiritual life and faith will not make your life problem-free, but you will come to learn there is a purpose and meaning for your existence. And when you know that, you can make a difference.

Best known for the Nobel Peace Prize, Alfred Nobel was a Swedish chemist who helped to develop dynamite. Through his scientific genius, he was able to make a fortune designing various explosives for construction companies and for the military. When his brother died, a local newspaper accidentally printed Alfred's obituary instead, describing him as a man who made it possible for men to kill large numbers of people at a time.

Shaken by this short assessment of his life, Alfred committed to leave a different legacy, and devoted the rest of his life and fortune to award those brave men and women who benefited humanity by bringing peace and reconciliation into the world. It is never too late to start today.

Mark Twain said, "I can teach anybody how to get what they want out of life. The problem is that I can't find anybody who can tell me what they want." Many people find it useful to perform an imaginary life review to gain clarity on what is most important. Envision yourself looking back over your choices from the perspective of a retiree during the final years of your life. If you continue living every day just as you are now without making any changes, when you review your life, what do you see? Is there love, rich laughter, vibrant health? Or do you seen pain and regret?

Now picture having lived the life of your dreams. Who is with you over the years? How do you spend your days, weeks, and months? Who do you impact? Did you paint a magnificent picture, craft a beautiful song, and learn to give more to others? As you see and feel the richness of those years, commit to doing now what you must do to create what you see.

I did this test a number of times with inmates who were about to be released. First, we would talk about where they would be in five years if they did not make any changes, and without fail, each one said they would either be back in prison or dead. Then we would talk about what would be their ideal life. They would light up as they talked about love and family, starting a career, and making up for lost time.

Ultimately, the choice was up to each one of them, just as it is up to you and me. As Lakhiani highlights, "The single most effective model of reality you can adopt right now is the idea that your models of reality are swappable. You do not have to continue believing and seeing the world through the lens installed within you in your younger years."[18]

Some of the changes necessary will require a lot of effort; some of the changes will be simpler. It might mean giving up things like sleep and entertainment. We live in a culture where the average person watches close to *fifty* hours of television a week. As Jim Rohn said, "Poor people have big TVs. Rich people have big libraries." Rohn often encouraged people to consider how much their television cost—not what each person paid for it, but what it cost in loss of time, loss of quality relationships, and loss of personal growth.

Studies show that only 10% of people who buy a book read past the first chapter, and only 3% of people have written goals, but those 3% are the most successful in pursuing and achieving their dreams. It is all about becoming part of the few who "do" versus the many who simply talk. But to be more, have more, and do more, we must be ready to make the sacrifice.

Perhaps you simply want to be a better husband, wife, parent or student. Maybe right now, your goal is to move forward in your career so you have more to give, or to get in better shape so you can have the energy required to better serve. Each of us needs to examine where we are, and where we want to be, and determine the best steps to get there. Always keep in mind, "If you are not contributing, you are not growing, and any organism in this finite existence that is not growing is dying."[19]

Steve Jobs would wear the same outfit every day: jeans, a black turtleneck, and New Balance sneakers. The genius billionaire behind Apple eliminated tedious activities from his busy schedule so he could focus on more important issues. A number of writers have credited Einstein with the popularity of red doors. The scientist is said to have painted his door red so he could effortlessly remember which house was his, freeing up his mind to focus on his theories.[20] Many define leadership as influence. But to influence others, we must first become self-leaders who do the work to make positive changes in our own lives, often doing what is uncommon.

Joel Andreas noted that statistics have shown that "in some inner-city high schools, 80% of the students drop out."[21] The government is not going to come to the rescue. Throwing more money at problems or writing more prescriptions to dull the pain will not shift our culture or our lives. Religion does not contain sustainable solutions. What will make a difference is high character and authentic faith followed by real action. It will require committing to live life consciously, and to uncovering the truth to the big questions we all have. The gospel message is not given to rescue you from the earth, but to rescue the earth through you! As Jesus said, "Everyone who is committed to the truth listens to my voice."[22]

The writers of the New Testament chose a secular word from the Greek when describing the message of Christ: *evangelion*. Bill Jackson notes the word contains the meaning of a *holiday* or a *celebration of a noble birthday*, indicating that authentic faith is meant to be a joyful celebration beyond *mere* living, even in the face of giant odds.[23]

In the fourth century, Augustine, an infamous adulterer, would surrender his life to God, eventually becoming one of the most studied authors in history. He had his own ongoing struggles with infidelity. Desiring to live beyond a mediocre faith, he wrestled in prayer, "Lord make me chaste — *but not yet.*" Tellingly, Augustine struggled with making one of the most important steps to creating real change.

The gospel writers summarize the first message of Jesus in only *eight words*, "Repent, for the kingdom of heaven is near."[24] The word *repent* means to turn and go the opposite way. The idea carried in the word indicates a complete change of behavior, thinking, and direction by choice.

If someone is selfish, they need to purposefully practice acts of selflessness. If someone is greedy, they need to choose to give to others without asking for anything in return. If someone has wronged another, they need to make recompense. For a person who loses their temper, they need to begin treating others with kindness. Carl Jung understood that what you resist will persist. If we continue to ignore problems, they will simply grow. To procrastinate making changes only exacerbates the issues. There is always a way if we are committed, willing to repent and willing to change course.

Peak performance coach Joseph McClendon notes that we are born with three needs: to avoid pain, to pursue pleasure, and to grow and learn.[25] He often shares that life is much simpler than we have been led to believe, and if we focus on basic principles, we will experience massive change. What stops us from living the life we were created for is all the noise in our mind telling us why we can't have it.

Those types of thoughts can be devastating. As Morrow notes, "Every thought the human mind has, immediately produces a chemical equal in response to that particular thought. Based on the intensity level of the event or given set of circumstances, the individual or group of people under such conditions will produce a common chemical bond synonymous with those events."[26]

Our habitual thinking helps to determine our behavior. Psychological studies show how strong this reality is by testing subjects with the "think-drink effect." I was stunned when I was able to witness this experiment. If you tell a group of people they are drinking alcohol but you give them non-alcoholic drinks, they will against all common logic still become intoxicated simply because *they think they should*.[27]

Our thoughts, whether empowering or disempowering, become a part of our nervous system. In neuroscience, it is the principle of "nerve cells that fire together, wire together."[28] Once a thought is born, if we relive it, then it becomes easier to repeat it the next time, and this process continues unless it is interrupted with a different thought. For example, some people have become experts at anger, and if you were to map their brain, you would see they have clear neuropathways developed around angry thoughts. On the other side of the coin, someone with thoughts of love will experience the opposite default traits and be able to more easily access the state of love.

Our thinking can either energize us or exhaust us because the brain consumes 16 times the energy of other muscles, consuming as much as 24% of a person's energy needs.[29] Repentance includes taking each thought captive and submitting it to the will so that our thinking comes in line with our true dreams and desires. In the following pages, we will visit a number of tools and strategies to take thoughts that no longer serve us and turn them into thoughts that move us towards our highest identity.

Aristotle said, "Happiness is the meaning and purpose of life." Yet, joy escapes many people because they fail to have consistency when it comes to the foundational practices that create a meaningful life and a vibrant spirituality. As Maxwell Maltz said, "Self-discipline is your golden key; without it, you cannot be happy."[30] Indeed, research of successful people has confirmed that self-discipline is a key factor of true fulfillment; it is *the* character trait shared across the board by achievers.[31] Too many people give up doing the necessary work needed when in reality, they are very close to the breakthrough their heart desires.

A better response to the challenges of life is found by the American buffalo. When a storm is on the horizon, the buffalo runs *towards* the thunder and lightning. By running into the storm, they quickly pass through the other side. Cows, on the other hand, run from the storm, which means they end up going in the same direction as the rain, so the herd ends up spending more time in bad weather.[32]

Is your spiritual life dull? Make it your mission to diligently investigate history to find some of the best examples of men and women who will challenge you to have a whole new mindset and to live life in a different direction. Begin to imitate the daily rituals of people who inspire you, then decide what changes you most need to make and start doing the necessary things that will move you towards your ultimate goals.

Classical pianist Arthur Rubinstein said, "If I do not practice for one day, I notice. If I do not practice for two days, the orchestra notices. If I don't practice for three days, the audience notices."[33] Begin with a daily commitment to move beyond mediocre and start doing the things that need to be done, and stop doing the things that need to exit your life.

Milton Erickson was a therapist who was able to produce legendary results when counseling individuals as well as groups. One day, Erickson met with Olympic rifle team members, wanting to more fully understand the psychology of success. He asked the group if they could hit a bullseye on their first attempt. Each person agreed they could. He then asked if they would be able to hit five bullseyes in a row, and they again confidently agreed it would not be a problem. However, when he wondered aloud if they could hit ten or fifteen bullseyes in a row, the majority of them said they doubted they would be able to.

His fundamental question was what was the difference between hitting the bullseye one single time, or of hitting the bullseyes one single time ten times over? The mechanics of each shot were the same; what changed was the confidence of the shooter. It was their internal dialogue and whether or not they believed they could that limited them.

His study highlights the power of belief about what is possible. For instance, a couple facing divorce could most likely agree to avoid arguing for one day. Ask them to do that same thing for 30 days in a row, and many would say it would be too difficult. What inhibits us is our own uncertainty about being able to produce a desired result. If we don't believe, then we are defeated before we even take the first step, or worse, we won't even try.

As Tony Robbins states, "Our beliefs are like unquestioned commands, telling us how things are, what's possible and impossible and what we can and cannot do. They shape every action, every thought, and every feeling that we experience. As a result, changing our belief systems is central to making any real and lasting change in our lives."[34]

Remarkable research has been done with two groups of people: lottery winners and paraplegics. Both groups thought their circumstances forever altered their lives for better or for worse. In reality, lottery winners discover the high wears off in a matter of months, and many who become paralyzed and wonder if they will ever be happy again find that the grief disappears. Incredibly, studies show that both groups found that "on average, a year after these dramatic changes in their circumstances, they gravitated back to their original set ranges of happiness."[35] This clearly indicates that it is *not* circumstances but our daily thinking, beliefs and rituals that produce or inhibit our happiness.

During the nineteenth century, a young woman named Charlotte Elliott struggled with numerous health problems. She was close to her brother, who was a minister, and wanted desperately to be able to help him as he served their community. However, as an invalid, she was constantly tired and often unable to leave the house. Though her brother sought to encourage her, she felt more and more hopeless, believing she would forever be ruled by her illness.

One day, a visiting evangelist dared her to do what she could to help other people from her home. When she lamented her illness and expressed her limitations, he told her, "Just come to him as you are."

That night, Charlotte went home, put pen to paper and wrote the following:

Just as I am, without one plea
But that Thy blood was shed for me
And that Thou bid'st me come to Thee
O Lamb of God, I come!

A century later, a young Billy Graham would take this same song as his signature hymn as he traversed the globe; the words of Ms. Elliott were sung around the world, bringing comfort and hope to millions of people who had wondered if their most useful days were behind them.

It is never too early or too late to start fresh. Anyone can simply choose to change the direction they are taking in a moment of decision, never knowing the impact such a seemingly simple step will make.

One place to begin is to have a regular practice of gratitude—a life-changing characteristic. As Kurek Ashley notes, "If you look at Jesus' life, you'll see he had unwavering faith that he could perform miracles, and he achieved that unwavering faith by thanking the Creator in advance of receiving the gift. He would say things like, 'Thank you, Father, for giving me the power to heal this person.' That gratitude gave him unwavering faith that he could perform the miracle and then he went and did just that. And remember: Jesus also said, 'Even the least among you can do all that I have done, and even greater things.'"[36]

At any moment, you can simply stop and give thanks for a heart that beats 100,000 times a day without any effort on your part.[37] With every powerful beat, it delivers life-giving oxygen to each cell in your body, moving nutrients through your entire circulatory system in 30 seconds. The human body has approximately 5 quarts of blood circulating 20 *billion* cells through the body 5000 times every 24 hours[38]—each moment is evidence of God's provision and care. On every one of your fingertips, there are a *trillion* atoms.[39] For this, the psalmist would sing, "I am fearfully and wonderfully made."[40]

Emerson wrote, "The gods we worship write their names on our faces, be sure of that. And a man will worship something—have no doubt about that, either. He may think his tribute is paid in secret in the dark recesses of his heart, but it will come out. That which dominates, will determine his life and character. Therefore, it behooves us to be careful what we worship, for what we are worshiping we are becoming."

Worship can simply mean *to give importance to*. If we continue to give importance to fear and scarcity, if we continue to give breath to doubt and negative thinking, if we continue to hold on to the past while failing to change direction, we can be sure our life will be far less than it is meant to be.

On the other side of the coin is life, light, laughter, and fulfillment. Change may not come easy, but that is what helps us grow. Moving in a different direction has its uncertainties, but we can trust there is no such thing as failure, only lessons to be learned, and as long as you take a step with a heart of integrity, you will see positive changes in your life. You don't have to have everything figured out ahead of time. That is why Augustine offered, "Love God and do the next thing." Simply step out into the unknown and trust your path will be revealed to you as you move in a new direction. You don't have to know all the answers to begin creating the life you have always wanted.

For those who are married, this is especially important when it comes to your marriage. However, for many, this is a place where they are barely keeping their heads above water. Weddings are a $51 billion dollar industry in America, with roughly 3 million taking place annually. Some 70% of marriages are held in churches, yet divorce rates remain at alarmingly high levels with many relationships held together with little love. Though couples may start off with a spiritual bond, it often dissolves the further they get from the sanctuary in which they made their commitment, and the further they get from being the person they said they would be when they took their vows. Sadly, this condition is much different than what was intended, so beautifully captured by Pablo Neruda, "I don't know any other way of loving but this, in which there is no I or you, so intimate that your hand upon my chest is my hand, so intimate that when I fall asleep, it is your eyes that close."[41]

How important is a healthy spiritual bond in marriage? In a stunning study by Gallup Research, it was found, "For couples that pray together every night, the divorce rate goes from a staggering one in two to just one in 1052!"[42] (Consequently, one of the best pieces of advice I ever received about prayer is that if you find it boring, it simply means you are praying about something you don't care about, so pray for things that you are passionate about.)

Countless marriages fail because partners fail to meet, or even care to meet, their spouse's most intimate needs. They no longer see their partner with the same eyes as they did on their wedding day. Is your marriage hurting? When together, do you elevate the status of your husband or wife in front of others, or do you tear them down? Perhaps one or both of you need to consider making a 180-degree change.

For example, Sue and Mike Dowgiewicz note that we are born with the need for security, defined as "confidence that we will experience protection and relational warmth."[43] Simply ask yourself, *how much security do I give to my partner on a regular basis?* As an anonymous person said, "We control fifty percent of a relationship. We influence one hundred percent of it."

Shalom Arush, widely considered one of the best marriage counselors in the Middle East, shares that for husbands, two of the most important keys to a successful relationship are to spend an hour a day in prayer for the health of your marriage[44] and to never criticize your wife.[45] It is about leaving behind the boy and becoming the man you are not only meant to be but secretly *crave* to be. One of the earliest texts in scripture says a *man* is to *leave* his mother and father and be united with his wife.[46] As David Deida expresses, "You don't need Mommy anymore, telling you what a good boy you are. And your woman doesn't want you to need mommy. In fact, it sickens her."[47] What she needs is for you to step up and show up daily with strength and integrity.

For a wife, know that your man lives for significance, which is why so many movies and myths contain a hero overcoming the dragon or the giant or impossible odds to win the girl. In that same vein, criticizing or belittling him will drive him away faster than you can imagine. Incidentally, John Gray offers, "There is no greater gift that you can give a man than giving him a task that he can carry out for you or that he can accomplish. A man bonds through action...but he needs to know what will make a difference to you."[48]

Tom Marshall affirms that we are all born with two needs: the need for love and the need for significance.[49] The key to relational health is meeting these needs for one another unselfishly. When it comes to love, it is about feeling safe, knowing we can trust our partner has our best interests at heart. It has been said that real friendship is when someone can see us at our worst and still like us. This should never be truer than in a marriage. When it comes to significance, if someone believes they are third or fourth place on another person's list, nothing but pain in that relationship will result. When husbands and wives put other family members, be it parents or even their own children, above one another, the relationship is in serious trouble. Nowhere in scripture is a connection between two individuals given greater importance than in a marriage where each partner is to count the other as first,[50] and be ready to sacrifice completely for one another.[51]

International family therapist Cloe Madanes notes that at any moment, we are making a decision about what to focus our attention on and what meaning we give to our interpretation of the events that occupy our thinking.[52] What do you focus on when it comes to your spouse? As Cindy Trimm states, "Whatever your predominant focus is, that is what you permit to exist in your life."[53] Negative focus produces the same in your life in marriage; positive focus will produce the opposite. Also consider what meaning you give to your shared story. Will you choose to live from a place of love or a place of anger? As Sister Corita said, "There's a positive side and a negative side and at every moment, you decide."[54]

Do you fight with your husband? Commit for the next 21 days to do the opposite and learn to listen without reacting. Do you have resentments towards your wife? For the next 3 weeks, practice meeting her needs at a high level while asking nothing in return. Place the other's wellbeing above your own. Remember how you felt and what thoughts took up space in your brain when you first said "I do," and return to doing the same things you did at the beginning of your courtship.

There is an ancient parable whose origin and author are unknown. In the story, two friends are walking through the desert. At some point, they have an argument, and one friend slaps the other. The one who got slapped was hurt, but without saying anything, wrote in the sand: "Today my best friend slapped me in the face." They continued their journey until they came upon an oasis, where they stopped to rest and to take a bath. The one who was slapped got stuck in the mud and started to drown, but his friend saved him. Safely on shore and recovered from almost drowning, he took a stone and wrote on it, "Today my best friend saved my life."

The friend who had slapped and saved the other asked him, "After I hurt you, you wrote in the sand, and now, you write on a stone. Why?" His friend replied: "When someone hurts us, we should write it down in sand where winds of forgiveness can erase it away. But, when someone does something good for us, we must engrave it in stone where no wind can ever erase it." So it should be in our most important relationships, where we commit to give more than is expected.

Some people need to change direction when it comes to their health—to stop eating the things they have been eating, to stop stressing over the things they have been holding onto, and to begin using their body and their emotions in ways that will best serve them and their future.

In the United States, some 13 *billion* pills for stress and depression are consumed annually. Though Americans are 5% of the population of the world, we consume 80% of all painkillers.[55] Toxic emotions like fear and anger trigger roughly 1400 chemical reactions and 30 different hormones in the body, leading to illnesses of every kind.[56] Incidentally, over three-fourths of all visits to doctors are stress-related.

One lady recently shared that her father had numerous health problems, many of them brought on by consuming excessive quantities of fast food. When the doctors told him his health would improve greatly with a new nutrition plan, he began to weep and plead that they not take away his fast food—his one comfort in life.

In the fifth century, Hippocrates said, "Let food be thy medicine and medicine be thy food." One couple I counselled said, "Look, we know we should *eat to live*, but we would rather *live to eat*." Extremely obese, they had let things go for so long, it was now painful just to walk to the car; however, they continued to move in the same direction they had always gone because the familiar was comfortable, even if it was unhealthy.

Freud didn't believe most people wanted to change, no matter how miserable they had become by the time they reached his office. His goal was to move people from "neurotic misery to one of common unhappiness."[57] Most just wanted to talk about their problems without doing anything to make a shift in their lives.

People who refuse to face unresolved hurt or emotional wounds are flirting with disaster. They are literally being poisoned by their environment, both internal and external. Dr. Theodore Rubin explains some of the physiological impact of failing to address destructive feelings and psychological wounds: "The ears receive sound waves. The eyes receive light waves that convey messages to the brain in which is integrated information that makes us angry. This feeling is felt by the entire body. Messages are sent out by chemical changes in nerves so that various hormones are excreted: heart-rate changes, the diameter of blood vessels change, and so on. These effects in turn affect the skin, musculature, the digestive tract, the lungs—all the systems and organs of the body. Messages that are smooth and free flowing will see healthy expression, messages that are polluted will have poisonous physical repercussions."[58]

One wise professor insightfully responded to the question, "If change is easy, then why don't more people change?" His answer? "Because it is easy *not* to change." We need to find a hunger to become better and move beyond average.

Anthony Robbins states, "Most people's lives are a direct reflection of the expectation of their peer group." It is imperative that each one of us becomes intentional about who we spend the most time with, choosing an inner circle that will challenge us to be more than mere men, while limiting the contact we have with toxic people. As Charles Jones said, "You will be the same person in five years as you are today except for the people you meet and the books you read."

Hericletus noted during war in 500 BC, "Out of every hundred men, ten shouldn't even be there, eighty are just targets, nine are the real fighters, and we are lucky to have them, for they make the battle. Ah, but the one, one is a warrior, and he will bring the others back."

Each of us can choose to be that one warrior, to lead by our example, to change the things that need to change, to do the things that need to be done, and to stop doing the things that are leading us away from "the life that is truly life,"[59] which is our birthright. Once we begin to see a newness in life and hold ourselves to a different standard, we can help those around us as well.

Montel Williams said the most important lesson he has learned in his entire life has been, "You alone are the person who owns the definition of who you are...I refuse to be defined by other people's limits, or their expectations, or their perceptions of me."[60]

Recently, while waiting in a slow-moving line for a restaurant, people began to introduce themselves. One woman, well into her golden years, introduced her two sons, both in their fifties. "This is my son James; he runs his own company," she said as she smiled. Then turning to her other son, leaning in to add emphasis, she offered, "And this is Walter; *he's the shy one.*" I watched as Walter's shoulders dropped along with his whole demeanor as she spoke, the pain of carrying such a label for decades. Sometimes, we have to move beyond what may be years' worth of other people's expectations.

As Ole Anthony notes, at birth you "are like an unprogrammed computer. The only things written on the computer program is what God originally placed there, but then your parents hit on the keys and type their programs. And then others, such as your relatives, your babysitters, your friends, your teachers, etc., program their input. By the time you reach adulthood you have a stack of floppy disks ten-feet-high through which all information is processed, and what comes out is totally different than what God intended."[61]

On his wall, Martin Luther had written the words to his favorite psalm,[62] "I shall not die, but live, and declare the works of the Lord." In his writings, he would express the message of the song in his own words, describing the impact of his faith in God and his belief in new beginnings, "The dying live; the suffering rejoice; the fallen rise; the disgraced are honored."

There is no limit to what can happen when a person simply changes direction, loves God, and does the next thing. Are you sick and tired of being sick and tired? Are you fed up with supposed support systems that fail to produce true contentment? Are you finished being labelled by others? The popular definition of insanity is only half true. The reality is that people continue to repeat the same actions, only when they don't get the results they want, they do the same things over again with *more intensity*. The idea is that if something is not working, try harder. But how has that worked out so far?

One effective strategy for making positive changes is to stop using word curses. Stating things like, "This will never change," or "I tried that in the past and it did not work," can create subconscious blockages. It is estimated that we have 60,000 thoughts per day, but for many people, they have the same thoughts each day: thoughts of defeat and despair.

What do we do to ourselves when we say, "I am not enough" or "I am a failure" over and over again, perhaps hundreds of thousands of times? The words you use make you feel a certain way; they create emotions. What you tell yourself on a consistent basis is everything. Moore and Gillette state, "Words, in fact, define our reality; they define our worlds."[63]

How powerful is your habitual thinking? Mark Pendergrast writes, "Psychologist Irving Kirsch notes, 'response expectancy theory' explains how 'when we expect to feel anxious, relaxed, joyful or depressed, our expectations tend to produce those feelings.' At its extreme, such a mindset can even lead to self-induced death as has been well-documented among tribes in which those under a powerful curse fulfill it by wasting away and dying, unless some way to reverse the curse can be found."[64] In modern-day vernacular, this phenomena is called *pointing the bone*. When a shaman or priest literally points a bone at a man or woman and declares a curse of death over them, if that person believes the curse is real, death often follows. Such is the power of conviction.

Numerous psychology studies have been done in which a group of people will take an unknowing subject at their office and over the course of an hour, they will tell this person, "You look sick; are you feeling well?" Then another person will stop and say, "You seem very tired; everything ok?" Before long, if this person receives these inductions without examining them using critical thinking, they will indeed begin to physiologically respond to the suggestions of the group and start to feel ill. As Morrow notes, "We must realize that once a certain thought is repeated in the mind, there is left in the chemistry of the individual a recorded imprint."[65]

On a personal level, Owen Fitzpatrick writes, "Think about what it would be like to have a constant companion who did nothing but insult you, made you feel bad for making mistakes, and filled you with worries about the future and regrets about the past."⁶⁶ For many people, this is exactly how their mind runs when on autopilot.

There is an old parable where two monks are walking through the woods when they come upon a young woman waiting by the river. One of the monks picks her up and carries her to the other side and sets her down on the bank. The two monks continue walking for several more miles until finally the second one says, "How could you have done such a thing? We took a vow that prohibits us from touching a woman!" The first monk responds, "Put her down. You are the one who is still carrying her." As Colin Wilson notes, "Most human beings carry a dozen invisible burdens."⁶⁷

One way to move out from under such weight is to begin to take the perspective we are given from a different, life-giving source. In scripture, Paul speaks of embracing a "high calling,"⁶⁸ while Peter defines your true destiny as "royal."⁶⁹ Rather than word curses, begin to speak of your identity in alignment with how the disciples described the faith-life. Learn to practice countering disempowering thoughts with superior statements and convictions. Understand as Fuhrman notes, "Words create feelings and feelings affect the way we behave."⁷⁰

Nigerian pastor Charles Ndifon offers a simple phrase to use when you are making changes in your life and the old thought patterns begin to come up; say out loud, "Mind, shut up!" After finding her life dramatically changed, one woman shared that the following day after making massive, even miraculous shifts in her mental and physical health, she had to say, "Mind, shut up" *every two minutes*, but as she stuck with it, she found herself overcoming her old, limiting thoughts of disbelief.⁷¹

Years ago, Emile Coue taught that people could cure themselves of various upsets and hurts in life, believing that people self-hypnotize themselves moment to moment by what they say and think. He suggested his patients repeat out loud twenty times first thing in the morning and again as the last thing at night, "Every day, in every way, I get better and better."[72] Doran J. Andry says a favorite of his to use on a daily basis is the Japanese word *mondai nai* (pronounced moan-dye-nye), which means "no problem."[73] Say it in the morning, say it at night, say it all day long, and say it when facing the fears and stress of life's demands until those disempowering emotions becomes a thing of the past.

As David M. Blunt shares, "Speak your expectation, not what you're experiencing. It doesn't matter what things look like. It doesn't matter what anyone else says. It only matters what God says—and what *you* say in response to Him. Hold onto your expectation!"[74]

To overcome his own giants, millionaire Dean Graziosi became a big believer in using power phrases. A favorite he recommends to loudly declare is, "If I can get through this, I can get through anything. If I can get through this, I can get through anything. If I can get through this, I can get through anything!"[75] It is all about doing the uncommon things to reach uncommon results. As Jonathan Royle notes, whatever your objectives, "Talk success, think success, act success, dream success and then successful things will occur."[76]

In like manner, Yuri Tereshchenko shares how to use the power of language when he writes, "Create a *picture* in your mind by what you *say*. If you do not feel good, do not speak that over yourself. Instead, declare, 'I am getting better.' Command your body."[77]

Psychologists estimate that about 50% of our personality and level of happiness is part of our natural makeup from birth. The rest is determined by the daily rituals in our thinking and in our actions. Ask yourself what you would do if you did not have any fear. "The secret," Price Pritchett shares, "is to manage the way we explain situations to ourselves—especially when we experience failure, difficulties, uncertainty, or loss, but also as we encounter opportunity or success."[78] How important is our attitude? A five-decade-long study of nuns found that those who were optimistic lived an average of *ten years* longer than their pessimistic colleagues.[79]

As Peter Ragnar notes, the story we tell ourselves about our lives, the movie we hold in our mind "comes with subtitles, which are your own conclusions about the rightness or wrongness of an event. These conclusions create an unconscious program that automatically injects certain emotions into your being."[80]

As a graduate of Robbins-Madanes training, I can assure you that repeating affirmations morning and night is a powerful strategy. When you find one that speaks to you, it is recommended you repeat the affirmation 50 times twice a day. Purchasing a simple tally counter will help you keep effortlessly on track. As Hall and Belnap note, using "see-hear-feel language over and over, eventually re-trains us to think in terms of behavioral evidences. This makes our goals more real and less abstract or vague."[81]

Creating your own affirmation around this language gives your brain specific perspectives to notice, something we will cover in more detail in the coming pages. For example, stated in the positive, you could simply say, "I see, hear, and feel the power of my new life," or "I see, hear, and feel the strength of unconditional love." For a health goal you could state, "I see, hear, and feel the energy of a healthy body" as you move daily towards a fitter you. As Hall and Belnap noted, the key is repetition.

Including physical movements—such as clapping your hands together, stomping your foot, or punching the air—along with verbal commands, produces much more rapid change than verbalizing a statement alone. This is one reason Anthony Robbins states, "Most of us realize that the way we feel emotionally affects the way we feel physically. But few of us realize how powerfully the reverse is true: when we are moved physically, we are moved emotionally, too. The two cannot be separated."[82] In fact, there is debate among scientists over which happens first: the emotion or the body's physiological responses (such as blushing or an elevated heart rate.)[83] By intentionally choosing to use a physical movement, you can influence your emotional state.

You want to stand taller than the problem. Like soldiers of ancient Rome who had spikes attached to their shoes so they couldn't be knocked off their feet,[84] we need to dig in and refuse to surrender to majority opinion, fear of rejection, memories that haunt us, or emotional patterns that no longer serve us. Clarity is power, especially when we define exactly what we want and what we will no longer accept in our life. As Caleb confidentially said, knowing what was rightfully his after his military victory, "Give me this mountain!"[85] It is this same type of assurance you need to bring to declaring affirmations.

One afternoon on career day at a high school, the military sent representatives to talk to the students about enlistment. At the assembly, each member was given 15 minutes to speak. However, the Air Force Staff Sergeant ran over his time, which led the Army Sergeant to do the same. The Petty Officer from the Navy also took this liberty, which left less than five minutes for the Gunnery Sergeant from the Marine Corps.

Quietly, he walked to the microphone, looked out at the students who were fidgeting in their seats, anxious to go to lunch. His voice boomed over the microphone as he simply said, "There are maybe 2 or 3 people here who have what it takes to become a

Marine. I will see those individuals at my table at the back of the auditorium in two minutes."

When the principal dismissed the students, the Gunnery Sergeant was mobbed by dozens of teenagers excitedly taking brochures and asking for more information on how to join the Marine Corps.

Sometimes, all that is needed is someone to point us in a different direction. Different standards, different life. Remember that, and you will go far in making positive changes.

CHAPTER 2

WHEN ALL THINGS BECOME POSSIBLE

"He never wrote a book...he never painted a picture or composed any poetry or music...he never raised an army...he had no formal education...his teaching lasted just 3 years...he set foot in just two countries...under his name in the Encyclopedia Britannica the entry runs to 30,000 words...he is by far the most controversial person in history...every recorded word he spoke has been relentlessly analyzed...His name is Jesus, and he presents an enormous problem for atheists."

– **John Blanchard** [86]

When skeptics ask for "proof" for the existence of God, one of the first places I point them to is Ken Gaub. When hurting people believe their cause is hopeless, or when someone's faith has taken a serious blow, I show them this story. There is no misinterpreting these events, there is no possibility of a coincidence, the odds are simply too astronomical. What you are about to read has the potential to change your life.

A part of a family musical group traveling the country, Ken began to question whether he should start a different career. Going from state to state ministering to the needs of others, he had begun to wonder if God was paying attention. His astonishing story unfolds in his book *God's Got Your Number*.

One day, as his group passed through Dayton, Ohio, heading to their next concert, his family suggested they stop for lunch. They pulled off at a busy exit. As everyone got off the bus to grab something to eat, Ken stayed behind to be alone with his thoughts.

Finally, he decided to grab a soft drink at a small restaurant he spotted down the road. He got off the bus, purchased a soda, and slowly headed back down the street to meet his family. His life was about to dramatically change with the ringing of a telephone.

As he passed a payphone in a gas station parking lot, it began to ring. Curious, he walked over, picked up the phone and said, "Hello?"

A voice replied, "Long distance call for Ken Gaub."

Recovering from his initial shock, his first thought was that he was being pranked. He looked around for the cameras, wondering who could pull off such an elaborate ruse. He tried to laugh off his surprise, but the operator sounded desperate. Several times she repeated that she needed to speak to Ken Gaub, and that this was no joke. As he told her the entire situation was impossible, another voice came on the line.

"Yes, that's him, operator. I believe that's him!" A woman from Pennsylvania began to tell him she was desperate for help, planning to commit suicide. As she was writing a final note before ending her life, in desperation, she had prayed that God would allow her to somehow talk to Ken Gaub, a man she had seen on television. She saw a series of numbers in her mind and called them.

For a moment, they both sat in stunned silence, knowing a miracle was taking place. She began to weep.

She went on to share that she thought she was calling California. He explained his office was in Washington, but that at the moment, he was driving through Ohio and had randomly walked past a phone booth in a gas station parking lot when the phone began to ring.

He counselled her, he shared the gospel, and she found peace and restoration by trusting in Christ. When he finally did hang up the phone, they both knew God was closely watching over their lives.[87] As the ancient words say, even at our lowest, we can know "underneath are the everlasting arms."[88]

It was Paul who would write, "All God's promises are "yes" because of Jesus the Anointed one – therefore, when we honor God, it is through Jesus the Anointed One that we say 'Amen!'"[89] Paul was saying that with authentic faith, the sky is the limit. But it is imperative that along with belief, we take action. For too many people, beliefs provide little more than a sense of comfort without taking any action.

For years, John Avanzini has taught the important principle, "God is not moved by need; God is moved by faith."[90] We *all* have needs, but Jesus made it clear he was looking for faith inside the people he encountered[91] at one time, declaring, "When the Son of Man comes, will he find faith on the earth?".[92] Likewise, Donald C. Mann notes, "Need does not move God or allow Him to move in goodness on the earth. God honors faith in him, not need."[93] Faith is what leads to obedience, which leads to action, which moves mountains. There, we move out in the knowledge and trust that God will meet us at our point of faith—a faith that is based upon the promises of "yes" and "Amen."

Recently, an abstract painting by Mark Rothko sold for $86.9 million.[94] A Jackson Pollock piece can move for well over $100 million. Yet, there is one image that has been declared "the greatest painting in the world."[95] In fact, this masterpiece saved a city from destruction.

In 1944, Captain Anthony Clarke, a tank operator from England, and his soldiers had surrounded the city of Sansepolcro, Italy. Believing Germans were hiding inside the buildings, they prepared to launch an attack. As Clarke surveyed the town from an elevated vantage point, he struggled to place the name of the city, knowing it was somehow important to history.

Suddenly, he was struck by the name *Sansepolcro*, and he remembered learning in school it was known to house the greatest painting in the world. Clarke had his men hold off the attack in fear the fabled museum would be hit and the picture destroyed. He ordered a cease fire, knowing he would have a hard time explaining to his superiors why he hesitated to follow orders.

The army waited overnight, entering the city the next day. By the time they arrived, the Germans had evacuated. Clarke's men quickly went to the museum and were relieved to find the work of art undamaged. The men stood staring, breathless, as their eyes fell on the masterpiece titled *Resurrection*, a fifteenth-century creation by the artist Piero della Francesca.[96]

The work depicts Christ triumphantly "emerging from the tomb with banner in hand, like a warrior who has defeated the enemy, the victory of life over death."[97] Soldiers have fainted at his feet, and his eyes are locked on the viewer, the desired of all nations standing tall as the King of Kings. His work and his calling are meant to compel us to a destiny of triumphant living as joint-heirs of Christ.[98]

Statistically speaking, belief in God has remained around 90% of the population in the United States for years. It takes little understanding to see the appeal of believing in a divine Father who loves us unconditionally, always has our back, and has rewards beyond measure waiting for us in the next life. But as James writes, "the devils also believe, and tremble."[99] His point is to question what difference a person's belief makes here and now if it is not backed up by action.

This doesn't only apply spiritually. I can believe that avoiding fast food and eating more fruits and vegetables is good for me, but unless that translates into eating healthy and changing my habits, believing does me no good. I can believe that exercise should be a priority in my life, but if I never pick up a weight or step on a treadmill, my belief is worthless. In point of fact, 30% of people that have gym memberships do not use them.[100]

If your beliefs have not moved you to make changes in your life, it is time to turn around and go the other way. The idea of countering such laziness and apathy was captured perfectly in a sign from a local gym that read, "If you look or perform the same as you did a year ago, and you're OK with that, get yourself out of this gym!" Change your direction, change your thinking, and change your life.

After conducting massive research on top achievers, Tim Ferris discovered one tool that "was the most consistent pattern of them all"[101] in 80% of the people who reached their dreams. It was to take at least 10 minutes a day to slow down their mind by quiet reflection or meditation. Four centuries ago, Blaise Pascal shared, "All of humanity's problems stem from man's inability to sit quietly in a room alone." During this time, many find it useful to visualize their goals already completed, or to focus on a verse of sacred scripture. It is also powerful to simply have gratitude in the moment. It is the choice between starting the day calm or frantic, between responding and reacting. Ten minutes helps to quiet our thinking, and since our thoughts help determine our action, it is imperative we choose them wisely at every turn.

I learned from personal mentors years ago the power of the right questions, both morning and night. When you consistently learn to ask a superior question, you will then find a superior answer. As Richard Bandler states, "When people start asking good questions, they get good pictures inside their heads. If you make a good picture, you will get good feelings."[102] From a positive state, we get better answers. Starting and ending the day with questions like, *what is a funny moment you remember, what is something you are most proud of, who do you appreciate, what is something you are most grateful to have experienced in life, what was the most meaningful lesson you learned today,* can radically change your life. Discussing them with significant people around you will help build healthier relationships. As Vaknin notes, write down a list of questions and "read the questions before you go to sleep so that they will be on your mind....Your brain is highly motivated to solve riddles. Asking good questions and giving it time to find the answers with no pressure, is one of the greatest talents you can develop."[103]

In scripture, the angel asked Hagar two questions worth regularly considering: "Where have you come from?" and "Where are you going?"[104] Cannon and Wilkinson offer two more transformational questions. The first one applies to key decisions you have made, such as your career, where you live, and how you spend your time. Quietly reflect and consider, "If I weren't doing this already, would I choose to do it?" The second question is, "When did I lose my sense of wonder?" along with, "How desperately do I want it back?"[105] Better questions lead to better answers and better outcomes.

(Incidentally, Mark Albion has some great advice to follow when it comes to careers: *keep your walking costs low*.[106] Things can go wrong a thousand ways in almost any organization, especially when you add in insecure leaders, so it is important to be wise when it comes to saving and investing financially. One day, you may find your life going in a completely new direction after divine prompting.)

Note the root meaning of two important words. The first is *enthusiasm*, which at its core means *god-like*. When we get excited, we are expressing the divine. On the other end of the spectrum is boredom. Boredom is the fast-track to depression. Interestingly, John Cage inserts, "In Zen they say, 'If something is boring for two minutes, try it for four. If still boring, try it for eight, sixteen, thirty-two, and so on.'"[107] If we can begin to appreciate something about the moment, the problem, the outcome, the lesson we found, then passion is born and boredom disappears.

The second word to consider is *desire*. The root meaning of desire is "of the Father,"[108] meaning constructive hunger for wanting more out of life is a *normal* God-given drive. Those who feel guilty about success, or don't believe they deserve a better life, will struggle to move their life to the next level. One thing to begin to believe is, *I deserve the life of my dreams*. Jesus said knowing the abundant life includes the promise that "your joy might be full."[109]

If you look to people who are fully alive, you will see they have different strategies, and they take action. If you do something you have never done before, you will see your life go through a growth process; it is the natural result of effort. In the process, you learn that success is defined differently by each person, and even when a goal is reached, it was the process, not the end result, that brought meaning. Indeed, part of the feeling of dissatisfaction of obtaining one goal is to push us to pursue deeper and more meaningful goals the next time. As Deida notes, "Each purpose, each mission, is meant to be fully lived to the point where it becomes empty, boring, and useless. Then it should be discarded. This is a sign of growth."[110]

Mother Teresa was once asked about her ministry outreach and how she would summarize the work they did in Calcutta, India. She replied, "We are committed to feed Christ who is hungry, committed to clothe Christ who is naked, committed to take in Christ who has no home—and to do all this with a smile on our face and bursting with joy...But the important thing is not to try to do everything...I don't have time to do everything...only those things pleasing to Christ."[111]

J. K. Rowling had clinical depression and lived on government assistance. She began to write a book at a small café because it was more comfortable than her apartment. Today, she is the world's first billion-dollar author, having written the Harry Potter series.[112]

Guillermo Maldonado wrote about a friend who was diagnosed with cancer. He told the doctor who gave him the diagnosis, "I do not accept it. I cancel those words!" Three months later at his next test, he was completely healthy.[113]

These examples express the importance of embracing *expectation*. What do you earnestly expect and believe God will do in your life today, tomorrow, over the next twelve months? How will that expectation expand your thinking? As Hank Kunneman wrote, "A spirit of expectancy and determination will get God's attention and cause Him to break through for us."[114]

Recently, a Harvard study revealed a sharp dichotomy between elderly people in America and China. In America, many people hold the *perception* that we *get old*—something they assume means growing weaker and losing vibrancy (it doesn't). In China, as people age, they are held in high esteem. What the researchers discovered is in America, older people had substantially higher rates of memory loss than those in China. In China, those in their golden years competed at the same level as much younger subjects, leading the researchers to note, "Each culture produced old people in keeping with the prevailing attitude about aging."[115] In short, their lives met their level of expectation.

Most people have heard stories of moms lifting cars off their children in a moment of adrenaline-rushed fear. In fact, there was much more to one of the original news stories than many people realize. The moment happened in the late 70s in Florida to a woman named Laura Shultz, who was 63 at the time. Her grandson was trapped underneath a Buick, and she lifted the back end off his arm. *Peak Performance* author Dr. Charles Garfield tried to get an interview with her, but initially, she refused, unwilling to talk about "the event."

Finally, after much convincing, she agreed to speak with him and said that she didn't like to think about what happened. She shared, "If I was able to do this when I didn't think I could, what does that say about the rest of my life? Have I wasted it?" Charles was able to coach her into pursuing her dreams. At 63, she went back to school and got a degree in geology and became a professor at a local college.[116]

All that happened the moment she took action and followed her dreams. You don't have to wait until you believe it is too late; you can make a difference today. Even if you have to admit you were wrong, make a phone call, give an apology, or any other thing. All the promises are *yes* in Christ; this is your birthright.

Part of the process of claiming what is rightfully yours takes place in your mind.

For unknown reasons to science, Monarch butterflies follow a very specific generational migration. Starting in Mexico, the first generation will fly to the southern United States where they will remain for life. Their offspring will fly to the central states, stopping somewhere around the Ohio River, where they will reproduce. At this point, the third generation will migrate to Canada to lay eggs. The fourth generation, born in Canada, will then take a miraculous flight all the way back to the same mountains in Mexico where their great grandparents originated from.

For countless years, this amazing insect has been following this same four-generation cycle, one of the most incredible yet misunderstood journeys in the natural world, almost as mysterious as the butterfly's transformation from an egg to an adult.

In scripture, Paul states; "Be transformed by the renewing of your mind."[117] The word Paul uses here for "transformed" is the same word we use to describe the stages of a butterfly's life: *metamorphosis*. This means that in the end, there is something completely different than there was before. This is how complete the change should be in our life when it comes to our thinking.

Writing about life after his own brush with death, Freddy Vest noted, "My natural thoughts run contrary to His image in me. They lean toward fear and selfishness and other worldly ways that oppose Him and the real me—my spirit. My mind will yield to my spirit, but only if it is continually renewed."[118] That is why thinking is so important, and why it deserves so much attention. But this has to be a conscious decision, with conscious effort.

Kurek Ashley shares, "The most successful habit, or success muscle, you can develop for yourself—the habit that will guarantee you the happy, healthy, wealthy, successful, fulfilled life you deserve—is the habit of being consistent and relentless in making sure you're constantly filling your mind with only positive, empowering thoughts. Remember that your thoughts are seeds, and whatever you plant determines what you will grow."[119]

What do you say to yourself on a regular basis? Are you more alive today or less alive? It is critical to use focused effort to replace completely any and all thoughts that no longer serve us with thoughts that are in line with who we want to become. As Emerson said, "What lies behind us and what lies before us are tiny matters, compared to what lies within us."

There is an ancient story about an old man and a horse. Historians debate its country of origin, but what is curious is that the parable is known around the globe. In the story, the old man owns a beautiful white stallion the king wants to buy. The people tell the old man to sell the steed to the king so he can become rich. "The horse is my family; I would never sell my family," the old man informs them. The people call him a fool and laugh at his moralizing.

The next morning, the horse breaks out of the stable and runs away. Gleefully, the townspeople gather in front of the man's house. "Stupid old fool, you should have listened and sold that animal; now your horse is gone. You could have been rich; now you have nothing."

The old man replied, "You don't know what this means; no one can know. Just say my horse is no longer in the stable; beyond that, we can't be sure." The people once again laugh at the old man and call him a fool as they walk away.

The next morning, the horse returns, and another other horse comes with it. The people in town are shocked. They gather in front of the old man's porch and tell him, "How lucky you are.

Your horse returned with another one; now you have two! You are truly blessed."

The old man replies, "No one knows what this will mean. Just say my horse has come back to the stable and another horse has come with him. Whether this is good or bad, who can say?" The people again snicker; the man is foolish they tell themselves; *of course he is lucky.*

The next day, the old man's son tries to train the new horse. Eventually, he is thrown from the saddle and breaks his leg. The people stand out front of his yard once again. "You were right to not be excited about the horses, old man. Now your son can't walk, and harvest is soon. You will have no one to help you with the farm. Perhaps, you are cursed after all."

The old man has grown impatient. "You people always judge. Just say my son broke his leg; whether this is good or bad, who can say?" The people leave once again convinced the old man doesn't know what he is talking about.

The following day, the country goes to war. All able-bodied young men are drafted into the army. The townspeople crowd around the old man's house. In tears, they cry, "You were right old man. Our sons are being sent off to war. Your son is not because he broke his leg. You both are so lucky."

The old man replies, "This is the last time I will speak with you. You never seem to learn. Just say my son is staying home; your sons are being drafted. What this means, whether this is good or bad, who can say?" With that, the old man closes his door; he never spoke to the people again.

We all have perspectives, and leaving them unquestioned is often the source of so many problems. When I was an undergraduate student, a missionary shared about spending time with a native African who was visiting him in America. They began discussing how different the cultures were when this African gentleman made an analogy. He shared that often Americans frowned upon his countrymen for eating with their hands instead of using utensils. He then continued, "Though you may find it odd that we eat everything with our hands, we find it strange that you have no problem eating at a restaurant and putting a fork in your mouth that has been used by hundreds of other people!"

Our perceptions shape meaning, which colors the way we see our past, present, and future. Mark Pendergrast notes, "In one sense, *we use words to tell ourselves the constantly reinvented story of our lives.* We are, preeminently, a species of internal novelists. That explains our insatiable desire to write and read imagined stories, which distill and interpret experience and render it meaningful."[120] Sometimes, the story we write, and believe we remember, is far from the whole truth.

In a famed incident many years ago, the first Dutch ambassador paid a visit to the king of Siam. The ambassador began to recount the history of the Dutch people, at one point discussing a winter battle where soldiers marched across a river that was frozen over. The king of Siam, who had never witnessed snow or ice, became angry and began to yell that it was impossible for water to be solid. He accused the ambassador of being a liar and had him thrown out of the court.[121]

While it is often said perception may equal reality, it is our job to question our thoughts and beliefs to uncover what is really true. As Griggs notes, "Perception does not exactly replicate the world outside...Our 'view' of the world is a subjective one that the brain constructs by using assumptions and principles, both built-in and developed from our past perception experiences."[122] And since we can change our perception, *what something means*, in a moment of decision, we have much more power than we realize when we direct our thinking, rather than letting our brain go on autopilot.

A few years ago, I listened as a speaker discussed a concept in psychology called *habituation*. Habituation simply means that if there is a stimulus we are constantly faced with, we become used to it. Eventually, we may no longer even notice it. For instance, a new lamp that buzzes will at first be very obvious, but after a few days, we will no longer consciously hear the noise. The same is true visually, which is why realtors encourage people to make note of small cracks and peeling paint when first purchasing a home. They appreciate that if the new home owners do not repair the wall upon moving in, soon they will stop seeing the imperfections. However, when they try to sell the house, the next buyer will notice them and demand they be fixed before closing the sale.

In light of the psychology of habituation, this person discussed depression, specifically questioning whether or not a person could be depressed for years. This is not to discount that some people have depression for long periods of time, or that some need professional help to cope with this condition. However, if a person feels an emotion on a consistent basis, just like the buzz from the new lamp, over time, they will become habituated to it and no longer experience it, at least not at the same intensity.

For example, if someone is crying, they will eventually stop, whether someone helps them or not. Biologically, we simply cannot stay in the same state for long periods of time without a change. Therefore, it is impossible to feel deep depression, or any other intense emotion, on a consistent basis for years on end with no break.

For the depressed person (or the angry person, etc.), it is more helpful to say that the person experienced depression at different times, with long periods of time in-between where they did not feel sad. In the end, a person who claims they have been unhappy for 10 years may in reality only have experienced depression for a total of 6 months. Those two periods of time are worlds apart.

Habituation applies to any feeling. I meet people all the time who will say they have been *angry for years* about some situation. In truth, they would visit that situation every now and then in their mind and periodically re-experience it. However, they did not do this constantly, so it is not accurate to say they have been angry for years. Rather, what they experienced was upset for a few minutes now and then, which may have only added up to a total of a few weeks. It is all about seeing things differently and being very careful and intentional about how we define a particular problem and how we tell ourselves the stories of our past.

A lot of couples who have trouble in their marriages have become conditioned to respond in hurtful ways. Habituated to their behavior, they may no longer even notice how they react to one another, having become stuck in repeating patterns.

There is a simple tool that can end this cycle and literally transform your marriage, no matter where it is. Called the "ten-minute rule," it requires that for the first ten minutes upon coming home, both the husband and wife show nothing but excitement to be together and discuss nothing but positive events. Both put themselves in an empowering state before coming back together, and if need be, they *fake it 'till they make it.*

When a wife comes home from work and says, "I have had the *worst* day!" you can be sure the tone being set for the night will be negative. When a husband walks in the door and begins ranting about politics or how much he hates his boss, the rhythm of the night has been set. It is far better to arrive home with excitement and a sense of playfulness before even walking in the door. Act out a passionate kiss from a favorite movie scene if need be, but change the way you respond towards one another and the feelings will follow. Had a bad day at work? It doesn't matter; change your thinking and your perception before you walk in the door. This is your birthright, to direct your mind and your thinking. As William James said, "The greatest discovery of my generation is that man can alter his life simply by altering his attitude of mind."

Are there times to talk about negative things? Of course, but not in a negative emotional state, and not when first coming back together. Are feelings important? Certainly, but we can't let our feelings determine our behavior. We need to live above momentary emotional reactions and have a different standard that says we will do the work when it is easy, when it is hard, when it is inconvenient, and when we don't feel like it. Indeed, Jesus challenged people who were living average lives, "What are you doing more than others?"[123]

True muscle is grown when you are feeling your worst, and you can find a better perspective, transform your thoughts, and freely give love. This is the way of the uncommon life, the pathway to living life on your own terms. As Bandler notes, "If you don't do things in your head to make your world more dynamic, it won't be."[124]

In the Middle East, it is known that camels hold grudges. Once a driver has mistreated one of these creatures, it will seek revenge. The locals have come up with a solution to this: they will place their clothing on the ground in the shape of a sleeping man. The camel will then take the first opportunity to trample the clothing. From that point on, the driver is safe because the camel has vented its anger.

In the same way, if we leave issues unresolved, there will come a time when they will show up, and the results can cause ultimate pain. That is why it is important to begin immediately using tools and principles that work. As Archilochus said, "We do not rise to the level of our expectations. We fall to the level of our training." It is so much better to live in the "yes" world scripture describes.

Following is a very useful strategy created by Nathaniel Branden for making a positive shift. He came up with a technique using sentence completion and what he labelled "sentence stems." The idea is to come up with 6 to 10 grammatically-complete endings to each stem. It is recommended you provide answers out loud as well as in writing first thing in the morning. After a week, it is helpful to review your answers and then begin using different stems for the next seven days. You can find many examples at his website.[125]

Branden suggested using four to six stems each day, and rapidly coming up with six to ten answers in two to three minutes. One stem that I find particularly powerful is, "If I were to take 5% more responsibility for my life and well-being..."[126]

Using this stem would look something like this:

"If I were to take 5% more responsibility for my life and well-being, *I would get up one hour earlier in the morning to exercise vigorously.*"

"If I were to take 5% more responsibility for my life and well-being, *I would pray for at least 30 minutes a day.*"

"If I were to take 5% more responsibility for my life and well-being, *I would take 15 minutes every evening to focus on what I am most grateful for in my life.*"

"If I were to take 5% more responsibility for my life and well-being, *I would plan and eat healthy meals each day to nourish my body so I would feel more alive physically.*"

"If I were to take 5% more responsibility for my life and well-being, *I would devote one hour a week to learning how to wisely invest my finances so my family can have a secure future.*"

"If I were to take 5% more responsibility for my life and well-being, *I would find a tangible way every week to let at least one person I care about know that I appreciate them.*"

There are limitless ways to gain personal insight with this tool. You can focus on a 5% change in your marriage, your health, your finances, your parenting or your career. The possibilities are endless, especially when you mix your answers with authentic faith, knowing that you are driven by something far greater than your own needs.

Belief has to translate into action; otherwise, what good does it do? We can cite creeds and constitutions until we are blue in the face, but until our actions are in alignment with what we say is in our heart, we are not going to see lasting changes in our lives or in our culture.

Like C. S. Lewis, I believe in following Christ as I believe in the sun, for by faith, I seek to see all things. But that faith has to translate into tangible steps of doing the work Jesus called his followers to do. As James wrote, "Show me your faith without deeds, and I will show you my faith by my deeds."[127]

Years ago, the world was moved by the power of such conduct when an Amish child was struck by a car and shortly thereafter died. As the police placed the driver of the car into their cruiser, the child's mother told the officer, "Take care of him." The officer assumed she meant her son and assured her the paramedics and doctors would do what they could. The mother then gestured to the man in the back of the police car. "I mean the driver. We forgive him."[128] Here, before the world, was living, breathing faith in action.

The author of the following is unknown, but the words ring solidly true:

> I had walked life's way with an easy tread;
> Had followed where pleasure and comfort led.
> Until one day, in a quiet place,
> I met the Master face to face.
>
> With station and rank and wealth for my goal;
> Much thought for my body and none for my soul.
> I had entered to win in life's mad race,
> When I met the Master face to face.
>
> I met him and knew him and blushed to see,
> That his eyes full of sorrow were fixed on me.
> And I faltered and fell at his feet that day,
> While my castles melted and vanished away.
>
> Melted and vanished and in their place,
> Naught else did I see but the Master's face.
> And I cried aloud "Oh, make me meek,
> To follow the steps of Thy wounded feet."
>
> My thoughts are now for the souls of men.
> I have lost my life to find it again.
> Ever since that day in a quiet place,
> I met the Master face to face.[129]

It is estimated that we take about 10,000 steps on average in a day, walking some 115,000 miles in a lifetime.[130] The question we must ask is what will we do with those steps? Where will we walk? Will we move towards a higher calling or will we pursue our own selfish ends? How will knowing the Master change our choices?

There is a remarkable challenge recorded in the ancient book of Isaiah. Six hundred years before Jesus would walk through Jerusalem, the prophet records the following words of Christ in anticipation of his crucifixion, death and resurrection: "He who vindicates me is near. Who then will bring charges against me? *Let us face each other!* Who is *my accuser? Let him confront me!*"[131]

It is a stunning declaration aimed at the devil who has held people spiritually captive since the garden. The tone is mocking. In modern-day language, he told the deceiver, "If you are so tough, then why don't you try giving it your best shot against me? You and I can go toe to toe. Face me, *I dare you.*" Scripture states the serpent had long kept people in a prison of fear and sin and death; here, Jesus makes it clear he was taking back all authority from the enemy and setting the captives free.

It is the same type of righteous anger Luke writes about when Jesus saw the fear in people's eyes at the death of Lazarus. Twice in the account, he writes that Jesus was beyond angry; first, when he saw his friends weeping, "he groaned in the spirit, and was troubled," and then again while standing outside the tomb of Lazarus, we read he was "groaning in himself."[132] The idea captured is that he was so angry, he was trembling. The intensity behind his emotion was palpable, so strong was his indignation against the accuser who continued to destroy and dominate lives through sin and death.

One day, we are assured the devil will be revealed in full, but it won't be like people imagine. Instead, we are told, "They that see thee shall narrowly look upon thee, and consider thee, saying, 'Is this the man that made the earth to tremble, that did shake kingdoms?'"[133] The cosmic bully will finally be shackled and put in his place. Until that day we are told Jesus stands between us and the enemy, daring him to make a move. As S. D. Gordon shared, "Prayer is repeating the victor's name (Jesus) into the ears of Satan and insisting on his retreat."[134] With Christ on our side, we have nothing to fear. This is why songwriter Fanny Crosby would say, "Don't pity me for my blindness, for the first face I ever see will be the face of my Lord Jesus."[135]

Sheldon Kopp stated, "All of the significant battles are waged within the self." It is there we wrestle with the internal voice that bids us to settle, to compromise, to dominate. Yet, it is there in the darkness that Jesus meets us, cleanses us, and shows us a new and empowering way to live.

It may take a 5% shift, or a 20% shift, but taking the right step, doing the next thing and showing our faith by our actions is how our life, and the lives of those around us, are truly transformed. Ultimately, it is about moving forward with the assurance that God's got our number.

CHAPTER 3

DECISIONS MAKE THE DIFFERENCE

"In the land of the blind, the one-eyed man is king."

– Desiderius Erasmus

In the 1930s, it is said that mobster Al Capone owned Chicago. He had an attorney named Easy Eddie. Capone took good care of Eddie, setting him up with a nice home. Eddie later had a son whom he loved to spoil.

When Capone eventually faced arrest, Easy Eddie turned the state's evidence against his former boss. Whether the attorney had an attack of morality or was simply protecting his own interests is widely debated amongst historians. Either way, Eddie knew he was taking a huge risk, and within a year of the trial, he was murdered. A poem was found in his pocket.

Eddie's life is often contrasted with another native of Chicago: a man named Butch O'Hare. A World War II pilot who was known for bravery, O'Hare received a Medal of Honor. Though from the same city, these two men had two very different lives.

It is often reported that upwards of 75% of lottery winners are bankrupt within 5 years. The reason is that until a person changes their belief system, it doesn't matter how much they have, they will still make the same decisions. A person living beyond their means on a moderate salary can just as easily live beyond their means after winning millions of dollars. Someone irresponsible with a little money can be just as irresponsible with a lot of money.

I listened to a speaker at a financial seminar share that if all the money in the world were evenly divided across the board, within a matter of months, all the cash would be right back to where it was before the experiment. Those who spend all their money would again be broke, those who save all their money would again build up their savings account, and those who wisely invest their money would once again be making profits, and the same division between incomes would return. While there are some financial situations beyond a person's control, his general point is well made. Those who spend it all would once again repeat the same mistakes and find themselves deep in debt. Those who understand how to use money instead of money using them would have greater incomes.

You can't simply change a context and expect a different result in someone's life. Core beliefs must change as well, then a person can take new actions consistent with their new identity. Otherwise, they will simply repeat old habits in a different environment. Research of millionaires bears this out as they show 90% of family wealth is gone with the grandchildren who fail to take the same views and work ethics of their predecessors.

One day, I was walking with a mentor who stopped to pick up some pennies on the pavement. He told me he appreciated that I did not make fun of him, as this behavior usually embarrassed his family. Then his tone turned serious as he said, "Years ago, a wise instructor taught me to never carelessly walk by money, ignoring something of value. Remember, *what you fail to respect will exit your life.*"

Just men and women have been tortured and unfairly thrown into prisons down through history. Inside the confines of the cell walls, they continued to live with love and compassion, changing the people they met inside. On the other hand, there are just as many stories of greedy and selfish people being given a second and third chance at redemption, only to later take advantage of the people who were trying to help them.

In each case, both groups lived in accordance with their beliefs and values. To change your life, you must be willing to examine your very core. When you work to change your internal environment and identity to align with divine truth, you recognize your royal worth and can begin to live accordingly. As Kenneth Copeland states, "The power of the new creation works from the inside out. It starts in your spirit. Then as your mind is renewed to what has taken place within you, your soul is changed. And as you increasingly grasp your true identity in Christ, your thoughts, words, actions and outward circumstances reflect that identity."[136]

When I worked with inmates, I tried to get them to see themselves beyond the label of a convict, and to embrace that they were a mother or father whose family was waiting on the outside and was in need of them to step up and be a hero. Each of us can nightly review the elements of our day and the outcomes we are producing and ask, "Who was I in this situation? What sort of person would I prefer to have been?"[137]

Zig Ziglar shared about a man who was waiting on the subway when a beggar walked up, selling pencils for $1 each. The man gave him a dollar and walked away without the pencil. A moment later, he went back to the beggar and said, "I want my pencil."

The beggar eagerly dug into his stash and pulled out a pencil and handed it to the businessman. When he did, the business man locked eyes with him and said, "You are a businessman like me. You are no longer a beggar." The words left a deep impact on the panhandler. Months later, this man found him, now pursuing his own career and reaching news heights of success. The former beggar told him, "Your words changed my life forever."[138]

We are not beggars, and we need to move beyond limiting beliefs such as these while realizing the transformative power of words, both in our own lives as well as in the lives of the people around us. You never know what a simple act of kindness can do to bless someone else. Indeed, as Moore and Gillette note, "Being blessed has tremendous psychological consequences for us. There are even studies that show our bodies actually change chemically when we feel valued, praised, and blessed."[139]

If you are ready to have a deeper spiritual life, you have to begin believing what a spiritual person would believe and doing what that type of person would do. Changing nothing means that nothing will change. Hope is not a strategy; taking action is.

Mike Bickle notes about growth, "We cannot consistently misuse hours each week and still have strong prayer lives."[140] The same applies for strong relationships, vibrant health, significant personal growth and financial independence. Changes have to be made with wisdom, by aligning our beliefs with what is noble and good. What area do you most need to work on? How will you schedule your time differently to address that need? Make a regular appointment with yourself to work on your goals. To simply leave up to chance for the mood to show up and to wait until you feel like it will only lead to failure.

This applies to relationships as well. Set up a specific time to discuss stressful conversations. This will leave the rest of your time with your loved one free from the pressure of addressing emergency after emergency. Rather than getting upset over situations, simply agree with your spouse that all serious conversations will be held on a certain night of the week. You will find this incredibly freeing as you begin to respond, instead of react, to the demands on your time.

One time, we had a certain person who was always wanting to complain about changes we were making at a nonprofit organization. She was not happy about anything, and she would constantly approach staff members to talk about what was supposedly upsetting her, keeping employees late when their shifts were over. After several days in a row of this, it became clear she was simply meeting her need for significance by getting a lot of attention with her negative attitude. I came up with a simple solution.

"You seem to have a lot of things you would like to discuss. We are glad to listen to them, so I need to you write them down on a list, and you and I will sit down for one hour on the 15th of each month to talk about each item. From now on, when you approach a staff member with a complaint, they will remind you of this agreement." We had one meeting, and she never complained again.

Cloe Madanes shared about a therapy session with a couple whose marriage was suffering because the husband claimed he was constantly feeling depressed and helpless. To stop the man from using his disempowering emotions to control his wife, he was given the directive to set his alarm every night for 3:30 AM. At that time, and at no other, he was to get out of bed and spend thirty minutes worrying. During the next session, the man said the instruction was too foolish and he only did it one time. However, he found himself sleeping great and did not bring up worry again during therapy.[141] It is amazing what can happen when you schedule your upsets!

You are the CEO of your life. Part of that responsibility is to use your time wisely, to make choices that align with wisdom and with your highest values, and to no longer live with a beggar mentality.

A few years ago, a woman I had never met knocked on my door. She heard I had been a pastor, so she had looked up my address. When I opened the door, she said we had a friend in common, and she was hoping I could help her with some money, as she had a flat tire. I handed her some cash and wished her well, knowing the entire situation was suspicious.

My concerns were verified the very next night when she called my phone. She said she must have the worst luck in the world because she had a *second* flat tire. I told her if she came to my house, I would help her.

A few minutes later, a friend dropped her off and I met her on the porch. "I have the worst luck," she said, smiling.

I looked at her and responded, "No, you don't have bad luck; you have an addiction." She turned to look at the ground, afraid to make eye contact, her smile now gone. "Do you have kids?"

"I don't see them much," she whispered.

"The man in your car, did he get you into this?"

"I don't want to talk about him."

As congruently and compassionately as I could, I told her, "Look, money and more drugs will not fix what is wrong, nor will they give you what you are looking for." She kept eyeing the ground, listening, so I continued, "I can help you, and some friends of mine can help you. But right now, you are facing one of the most important decisions of your life. Tonight could be the best night of your life. Are you ready to make a fresh start?"

She paused, then quietly said, "No, I am not." She got up and slowly walked back to the car where her friend was waiting, and they both drove away. I have never seen her again.

We all get what we tolerate. What will you no longer allow in your life? What standards will you uphold? What will you begin to do today to lead an uncommon life? As Jim Rohn would say, "You can't hire someone else to do your push-ups for you."

Another time, I was sitting in the church office when a large man knocked on my door asking for help. As he sat down, he began to weep uncontrollably, telling me his mother had just died. Though we had never met, he began to share about losing his job and having no money to travel back home for her funeral.

He was desperate, and he needed help. After we talked for a while, I told him I would gladly help him purchase the needed bus ticket so he could be back home with his family.

In thanking me, he began to talk about his own faith. He asked if we had a piano, and when I explained we had one down the hall, he said he wanted to share a song. Sitting down on the bench, with effortless skill, he played and sang a hymn about God's grace. We walked to the door and I handed him the money for the ticket as he wiped away a final tear and said goodbye.

Five days later, my secretary buzzed my line to tell me this man had returned. I have played this game long enough to know this spelled trouble. As I approached him in the hallway, he made a fatal mistake, "Remember me? You helped me last week when my father died."

I looked him sternly in the face and said, "No, I did not. I helped you last week when you told me your *mother* died." With a look of shock on his face, he knew he had been caught. I told him I would give him a three-minute head start before calling the police. He quickly exited the building and hurried down the street.

I have come to learn that sometimes, the people who are most vocal about themselves are the least to be trusted. In reality, they are often trying to cover up their own inadequacies or hidden vices.

Not long ago, I met a married couple who said they felt a divine calling to be musicians. Knowing I was a pastor, they wanted to talk about possibly networking with people I knew in the hopes of getting their careers off the ground.

There were red flags as I listened to them speak loftily about themselves, while in the same vein, criticizing other authors and singers for not being spiritual enough. There was a certain amount of arrogance that made me uncomfortable with every word they said.

I was little surprised when a short time later, the husband contacted me. His wife had left him for another man, and he was hoping I might be a character witness if things went to trial, as his wife was accusing him of threatening to kill her. From that point, they allowed their house to go into foreclosure, declared bankruptcy, and broke countless promises they had made to people in the community.

It is like the old axiom: if you have to tell people you are cool, then you are probably not cool. If someone has to loudly proclaim they are spiritual and a person of good character, there is a good chance they are neither one.

The New Testament is far less generous when describing people like this, labelling them as "stains in your fellowship...

with no scruples, looking out only for themselves...clouds without water...trees without fruit, twice dead."[142]

Unfortunately, because of how vocal they are, many people believe individuals like this represent men and women of true faith, while in reality, nothing could be further from the truth. This is even more of a reason to be a person who lives with integrity, to counter the bad examples that abound. Chesterton said, "When a man stops believing in God, he doesn't believe in nothing. He believes in anything." We need to be people who lead others to a deeper faith, not further from the light. Actions have consequences.

An anonymous believer from Africa shared, "I'm part of the fellowship of the unashamed. The dye has been cast. I have stepped over the line; the decision has been made. I am a disciple of Jesus Christ. I won't look back, let up, slow down, back away, or be still. My past is redeemed, my present makes sense, my future is secure. I'm finished and done with low living, sight walking, smooth knees, colorless dreams, tamed visions, worldly talking, cheap giving, and dwarfed goals. My face is set, my gate is fast, my goal is heaven, my road is narrow, my way is rough, my companions are few, my guide is reliable, my mission is clear. I won't give up, shut up, let up, until I have stayed up, stored up, prayed up for the cause of Jesus Christ. I must go till He comes, give till I drop, preach till everyone knows, work till He stops me, and when He comes for His own, He will have no trouble recognizing me because my banner will have been clear."

There is a statement of Paul that is often overlooked where he writes, he "exalteth himself... so that he as God sitteth in the temple of God, *shewing himself* that he is God."[143] Why does the old self have to *show himself* that he is God? Because no one else will.

Why won't anyone else? Because they are too busy trying to *show themselves* that *they* are God.

You and I are the temple, and it is our old self who wants to sit in the throne room where it doesn't belong. It is a picture of the height of arrogance and self-centeredness. There is only one who belongs in the throne room, and as long as we oppose him, we are in reality opposing our self, because he knows the true purpose of our life. It is an exhausting and unwinnable fight. It is far easier to get out of the way and let Christ reign *in* us, live his life *through* us, and show us the victory he has *already* gained on our behalf.

It is said there were no flies in the Holy Temple. Even though all day, long lambs were slaughtered and blood was spilt, no flies were there. Why? Because it was holy ground, and where there is holiness, there is no decay.[144] If you want to experience increase and abundance and true happiness, personal holiness must become a priority.

Unfortunately, what is revealed in too many studies is often the sharp dichotomy between what many people say they believe versus how they actually live. David Frederickson shares, "So you come into a church and it seems loving. But it's a veneer. When you get to know the people—they do the same thing in their marriages unbelievers do, they have the same troubles with pornography and divorce. In fact Christians have a lot of faults the unbelievers don't have."[145]

Things were not meant to be like this. Jesus said, "I have told you this so that my joy may be in you and that your joy may be complete."[146] Peter believed that disciples should experience "an inexpressible and glorious joy."[147] Clearly, Jesus and his followers taught that following his example would include noticeable changes to a person's life.

Hungry for the deep waters of authentic faith? What you are about to read is one of the greatest evidences of the reality of Christ.

Here is where things take an astonishing turn, both historically and spiritually.

In the Old Testament, the most important day of the year was Yom Kippur, also known as the Day of Atonement. It was on this day that the High Priest entered into the Holy of Holies where the Ark of the Covenant was sitting. This was the only day anyone was allowed to enter the coveted room. The priest would make a sacrifice for the sins of the entire nation.

The following confession was made: "O Lord, your people, the house of Israel, has committed iniquity, transgressed, and sinned before you. O, by the Lord, grant atonement, I pray, for the iniquities and transgressions and sins that your people the house of Israel have committed and transgressed and sinned before you, as it is written in the Torah of your servant Moses: 'For on this day shall atonement be made for you to purify you of all your sins; thus you shall become pure before the Lord.'"[148]

Two goats were used for this ceremony. One goat's blood was placed in a bowl inside the Holy of Holies as a reminder that sin leads to death. The other animal was marked as the scapegoat and was taken ten miles outside the city. The symbolic act of leading the animal far from the protective walls of the community painted a picture of sin being removed from the land.

A red strap was used to identity the scapegoat. The Talmud notes in stunning detail what happened next: "Throughout the forty years that Simeon the Righteous ministered, the lot ['For the Lord'] would always come up in the right hand; from that time on, it would come up now in the right hand, now in the left. And [during the same time] the crimson-colored strap would become white."

This miraculous changing of the scapegoat's crimson-colored strap from red to white was seen as God showing that the sins of the people had been taken away. In Isaiah we read: "Come now, let us reason together," says the LORD. "Though your sins are like scarlet, they shall be as white as snow; though they are red as crimson, they shall be like wool."[149]

It is important to pause and reflect on what is being related here. The Talmud records a *literal* change in the color of the strap that had been found in the high priest's right hand. However, what happened next is simply astounding.

The Talmud records, "Our rabbis taught: During the last forty years before the destruction of the Temple the lot ['For the Lord'] did not come up in the right hand; nor did the crimson-colored strap become white."[150]

The ancient texts here reveal something remarkable. The Day of Atonement had been celebrated for millennia, and for decades, under Simeon's leadership, a special miracle happened where the scarlet strap for the scapegoat miraculously turned from red to white, a symbol of spiritual cleansing.

However, *forty years* before the Temple was destroyed, the strap *stopped* turning white. History tells us the Temple fell for its final time in AD 70 on the *exact same day* Solomon's Temple had previously been destroyed by the Babylonians in 586 BC. This means the strap stopped turning white in AD 30, *the time when Jesus was crucified.*

In his dying breath, Jesus proclaimed, "It is finished,"[151] which literally means *paid in full.* (Tax collectors wrote this same wording on receipts to indicate a final payment and that nothing else was due.)[152] The reason the strap stopped turning from red to white is because Jesus was the final sacrifice and no more would be needed or accepted in the divine courts of heaven. All this was because the debt was paid in full.

Dr. Jack Hayford states, "*Tetlesthai*—it is finished! The most significant single word in the Greek New Testament translates to the most triumphant declaration! It contains both a prophecy and a verdict. On the cross, Jesus, the Son, anticipated the Father's verdict and His ultimate intervention. The dawn of the world's redemption had broken, and with it the chains of human slavery to sin, shame and condemnation were shattered."[153]

Hebrews states, "For Christ has not entered the holy places made with hands...but into heaven itself."[154] In the process he opened the gateway to enter into the eternal Promised Land, leading by example and by laying down his own life. This is why scripture speaks about a revelation and an experience of complete and inexpressible joy!

History tells us there were two very different outcomes for Easy Eddie and Butch O'Hare. The poem found in Eddie's pocket read, "The clock of life is wound but once, and no man has the power to tell just when the hands will stop."

While Chicago may have wanted to leave behind his memory, it chose to solidify Butch's. Butch had died a war hero, and to pay tribute, Chicago named their airport in his honor: O'Hare International Airport.

What is the connection between the two? Easy Eddie was Butch O'Hare's father. Decisions make all the difference.

CHAPTER 4

BREAKTHROUGH LIVING

"Live as if Jesus was crucified yesterday, rose from the dead today, and is returning tomorrow."

– Martin Luther

There is a fable about two brothers: one who is rich and one who is poor. The poor brother toiled in the fields all day growing turnips, one day growing a turnip so big that when he put it in a cart, it took two oxen to move it.

He knew this amazing vegetable was too grand to eat or to sell; indeed, such a grand work of art was fit to give to the king. The brother did that very thing. Marveling at the turnip, the king told the farmer he was very lucky.

The poor farmer replied, "No, I am poor and toil all day long. I have nothing and will be forgotten by all." Taking pity on this man who was so generous with his turnip, the king bestowed riches of gold and land upon him.

When the rich brother found out what happened, he imagined what great things the king might give him if he also brought a gift. So, the rich brother collected all his gold and horses, lavishing them upon the king.

The king was overwhelmed at the generosity of the rich brother. Wanting to give a special gift in return, the story reads, "The king took the present, saying that he could give nothing rarer or better in return than the huge turnip. So the rich brother put his poor brother's turnip into a cart to have it taken home."[155]

The story tells us about a conniving brother who ends up with a more or less worthless object because his motivation was greed. The selfless brother, on the other hand, was rewarded far beyond his dreams. In this fable we are asked us to consider why we do what we do.

Martin Luther King Jr. said, "If a man is called to be a street-sweeper, he should sweep streets even as Michelangelo painted, or Beethoven played music, or Shakespeare wrote poetry. He should sweep streets so well that all the hosts of heaven and earth will pause to say, here lived a great street-sweeper who did his job well."

There is a captivating story in the gospel where Jesus approaches a spring surrounded by sick people. The focus of the encounter is upon one particular man who is unable to walk. John writes, "One who was there had been an invalid for thirty-eight years. When Jesus saw him lying there and learned that he had been in this condition for a long time, he asked him, 'Do you want to get well?'"[156]

In the story, the man responds, "I have no one to help me into the pool when the water is stirred. While I am trying to get in, someone else goes down ahead of me."[157] Jesus heals the man, who sadly goes away without much gratitude, apparently using his new health to indulge in sin, something for which Jesus rebukes him later on.

"Do you want to get well?" It may seem the answer would be obvious, but things are not so simple. I have counselled many people who did not want things to improve. They wanted revenge, to nurse hurts and anger, to feed bitterness, and to indulge in sin.

I remember one particular woman who told me she really wanted to change, having grown tired of waking up in bed next to men whose names she couldn't recall. We spoke often about spiritual things. She became excited about her new-found faith, even reading scripture for a brief time. However, before long, she told me she was giving up this whole "God thing." I asked her why, and she simply told me, "I like sex too much." She then went back to indulging in one-night stands with various strangers, eventually becoming pregnant and shortly thereafter abandoned by the would-be father.

The rabbis taught that after the Fall, Adam and Eve went into a dark depression. Some sources say they were unable to bear what they had done, so the first couple sat in a dark cave for decades, unable to look at one another, feeling overcome with shame.[158] In a similar vein, early church writers speak of Judas as a disfigured wretch who smelled so bad people could hardly stand the sight of him, let alone the stench.

What these sources are trying to capture is the pain that sin and selfishness bring. As Wei Wu Wei said, "Why are you unhappy? Because 99% of the things you do, think, and feel are about yourself."[159] Sin and selfishness destroy life, and many are left sitting around the pool of pity talking about all the reasons things can't get better. As an anonymous believer said years ago, "Sin will take you farther than you want to go, keep you longer than you want to stay, and cost you more than you want to pay."

It is in those moments, Jesus offers, "Do you want to get well?" The Book of Romans declares, "Just as Christ was raised from the dead by the glorious power of the Father, now we also may *live new lives.*"[160] The true mark of a disciple is a changed life and changed motives.

In the fifth century, a monk named Arenius had left Egypt's cities to live a simple, holy life in the desert. When in Alexandria, he enjoyed walking through the marketplace. When his students asked why he spent so much time browsing the tables, he replied, "I'm allowing my heart to rejoice at all the things I just don't need."

In the new life, we can rest in him, taking no thought for tomorrow because we know he has already taken care of our needs for that time so we can live with peace today. In *The Secret of the Ages,* Robert Collier says, "There are hundreds of millions of stars in the heavens. Do you suppose the Mind which could bring into being worlds without number in such prodigality intended to stint you of the few things necessary to your happiness?"[161]

It was a common practice during the first few centuries of the early church to share a meal that included milk and honey after someone was baptized. These symbols of the abundance found in the Promised Land were used to represent the all-sufficiency found in true faith. The disciples were able to spread this faith throughout the Roman Empire in the first century as Rome had made travel safe by building tens of thousands of miles of roads for tourists. The paved roads were 20 feet wide and were populated by trained guards. Up until then, bandits and thieves had been a common source of danger.

The people of the day were waiting for the arrival of the *Messiah*, a word the Greeks translated as the *Christ*. Both words mean *anointed one*, indicating oil that is rubbed or poured upon the skin, a practice often reserved to designate a new king. The New Testament writers would state that in the past, divine revelation had been passed down through the words of the prophets, but now it had been fully revealed by God through "his Son, *whom he appointed heir of all things.*"[162]

The new king faced death threats from the moment of his birth. Herod would seek to murder all the infant boys in Bethlehem when the wise men of the day claimed the stars were aligned to indicate a royal birth in that small town. After Herod was gone, Jesus and the disciples lived most of their lives under the rule of Tiberius, known for exiling his wife to die on an island. When Tiberius died, Caligula took up the mantle of violence, killing most of his rivals to the throne, including his own family. He was eventually murdered by his followers, having been one of the first rulers who demanded the people worship him as a god.

Caligula had spared the life of his uncle Claudius. In exchange, Claudius married his own niece, adopted her son, and appointed him the next ruler of Rome. His name was Nero. The terror he wrought was the height of wickedness, violence, and perversion. A maniac, he murdered his own mother, and enjoyed using human torches for his parties while he dressed up in animal skins and assaulted his dinner guests. His favorite people to torture? The followers of the Way.[163] John would simply refer to this evil emperor as "the beast."[164]

To be a committed disciple often cost everything, but in return, one would receive that which supersedes time and space: the promise of redemption and of power for living victoriously in spite of life's circumstances. Ignatius, a friend of the Apostle John who was martyred for his faith, would write, "Jesus Christ… was truly born, and ate and drank. He was truly persecuted under Pontius Pilate; He was truly crucified, and truly died. He was also truly raised from the dead."

For these promises, early believers were ready to die. Luke would confirm that after the resurrection, Jesus "presented himself to them and gave many convincing proofs that he was alive."[165] Perhaps the greatest proof of all has always been changed lives.

When persecution of the church reached unbelievable heights under Marcus Aurelius in the second century, many believers were heartbroken when other Christians denied their faith to escape torture while leaving their brethren to be beaten and burned at the stake. When persecution ended, those who had turned their backs on the church to avoid punishment were labelled *Lapsi* for having lapsed in their faith when it was needed most. Wide debate arose as to whether or not those who carried the scars of suffering should retain close ties to those who had previously renounced their faith and who later wanted to return to the church.

Today, the vast majority of us face nothing to compare to such trials and tribulations when it comes to following Jesus. How much more painful it is in light of how safe it is to walk in faith, that those who claim they do often lead lives that suggest anything but. There are times I doubt believers from the first few centuries would recognize much of what is labelled as Christianity today. To imagine comparing disciples whose scars were the price of admission to worship against the backdrop of the average church goer of today—with their plastic smiles and starched shirts, lattes in hand, wondering aloud if anyone thinks the service will last more than an hour while complaining about the sound quality and the temperature of the air conditioner—would be laughable, were it not so sad.

I have listened as parents shared about changing churches with about as much thought as they gave to selecting a pair of socks. One mother gleefully told me she couldn't wait to move to the new church down the street because they had just installed a taller slide than the one on the playground of the church her family had currently been attending. Her shallowness reminded me of the words of Johnnie Moore who shared about spending time with persecuted believers in the Middle East. Under threat of death, these men and women looked awkwardly at the West, "perplexed why so many Christians are barely willing to live for what *they* are so willing to die for."[166]

Consider the strange but common practice for engaged couples to get baptized, take vows of commitment in front of a church, then never be seen again after the wedding is over. Wintley Phipps notes, "I have heard it said that men and women can trace their success or failure in life from the moment they said 'I do.'"[167] Yet many approach matrimony with a desperate flippancy. Why do we do the things we do? Do we want to get well? Do we believe that Jesus truly died and rose again?[168] Does our faith lead to a changed life, or is it something we fall back on for convenience?

Years ago, John G. Lake lamented, "We are such a weak, wobbly lot in these latter days. God is just trying to get some backbone in us. We come along and are baptized and about a week after, we can find them doing all sorts of things. The Christians in the old days came down to get baptized, and as they did so a Roman officer took their names and sent them up to Rome. Instantly their citizenship was cancelled, their right of protection from Roman government was cut off, their goods were confiscated, they were left as a prey to the avarice of the people, but they got baptized just the same. Bless God."[169]

In the last twenty years, church growth seminars have become more and more popular. I attended a few out of curiosity and in the hopes of learning valuable and actionable information. The quality of the content was simply not what was advertised.

I took note as various speakers claimed their congregations had experienced massive growth after canvassing neighborhoods and taking surveys of what people would like to see most in a church. After these conferences, countless ministers went back to their congregations and began to build better nurseries, integrate new styles of music, and talk about "safe" topics on Sunday mornings in an attempt to be more relatable to their listeners.

The outcome? A lot of time and effort were put into temporary changes that produced very limited impact. Studies show these tactics produce measurable results in a *very* small fraction of churches.

Finally, at one of these seminars, the lead lecturer offered to speak with attendees between breaks. I hesitated to engage this person, but after he was sitting alone at one of the breaks, I approached him.

"I don't believe most of these ideas are transferable," I told him. "I believe they worked for you because you were starting a brand new church, and people often enjoy going to grand openings of almost anything." I explained that while I fully trust in divine providence, I imagined most of the ideas he presented worked in a very select group of churches by sheer *luck* because marketing is effective in select cases, which is why companies spend millions of dollars on commercials. He looked at me for several moments before responding. All I can say is, he didn't *disagree*.

But what about sustainable answers that move people from apathy to action? Ronnie Floyd writes, "You will never be any greater than your own personal walk with Jesus Christ."[170] Until we begin to live from the internal promise of knowing and experiencing Christ, placing him before all other things, our lives will be only as committed as we feel like in the moment.

In the late nineteenth century, Mel Trotter was a hopeless alcoholic. When his child died at about three years old, Mel threatened to commit suicide, saying it was his fault because he couldn't control his drinking. He wept as he decreed to his wife that he did not deserve to live. He did not follow through on his threat, and minutes after the funeral for his son, he was drunk again. Broken, wanting to die, he wandered the streets of Chicago until he came upon a small gathering where a man was testifying to God's power to deliver the addict. That night, Mel gave his life to Christ and was made whole for the first time in a long time. He eventually headed up missions to help other alcoholics find freedom. When asked how he knew that Jesus delivered him, he responded, "I was there when it happened. January 19, 1897, 10 minutes past 9, Central time, Pacific Garden Mission, Chicago, Illinois, USA."

An old adage states that winners don't need to make excuses why they won the game, while losers are full of excuses for why they lost the game. The time for excuses is past; now is the time to commit fully to focus on growing and living faith with the intensity of a trained athlete pursuing a victory.

In AD 320, Emperor Licinius demanded his Roman soldiers make sacrifices to the local gods. Forty refused because they were disciples of the risen Nazarene. In response, the emperor had them thrown naked into a frozen lake. He had fires and warm baths placed outside the water, and he offered warmth and redemption to each one if they would surrender to his demands.

Throughout the night, the men sang hymns and encouraged one another to not give up. Finally, one man said he could not take it any longer and rushed to the shore and into the warm bath. The emperor smiled in victory. But it would be short lived.

Suddenly, another soldier on the banks of the water stated that there were forty men in the lake, now there were thirty nine, and it should not be so. "I am a Christian!" he shouted. He then undressed and joined the men in the frozen lake. All forty would die in the icy water.

Total commitment means to play full-on. To have a spiritually fit life means to look like Jesus in how we live, how we give, how we love, and how we respond to life's demands. Each of us can examine the previous six months and compare where we are today and simply ask, *am I more or less like Jesus? Why, or why not?*

It is said that the most costly advice is bad advice. Popular opinions are often the most destructive. We live in a culture where studies have shown that people thrive on negative news, despite their cries to the contrary. When media outlets include more positive stories, they lose viewers and readership declines sharply. (It is believed this is in part because we remember sad and shocking stories more easily than pleasant ones, a built-in self-defense mechanism of the brain made to take special notice of pain.) And while negative news may be more popular, does more popular make it right? Sometimes, the best advice is to watch what the majority of people are doing and simply turn around and go the opposite direction.

Artist Robb Armstrong shares, "We should never allow our fear—of failure, of looking silly, of anything—to stop us from following our dreams. Sometimes you have to take risks—and perhaps even fail—to get better."[171]

When I counsel couples before marriage, I advise them to make two lists; one is a list of *must haves* and the other is a list of *must not haves*. Until we get clear on what we will no longer accept in our lives, of what standards we will hold ourselves and the people around us to, we will face untold frustration as people unfairly cross our personal boundaries.

Paul states that "whenever anyone turns to the Lord, the veil is taken away."[172] The blindness to our own shortcomings falls from our eyes when we have been given spiritual sight. When we begin to see life from the perspective of Jesus, everything takes on a whole new dimension. We stop taking lightly why he suffered, and we begin to value what he values.

Robert Ingersoll was a lawyer and a veteran of the Civil War. He gave speeches about his own doubts in the existence of God. One day, before talking to a crowd, he received a letter from a former schoolmate who shared about his dramatic deliverance from alcohol. After almost losing his wife and children, this man found hope and restoration in Christ and his life was completely changed. He challenged Ingersoll to reconsider bashing the power of faith.

Ingersoll read the letter to the room full of people gathered to hear him that night. Pausing, he set the note down and responded, "Ladies and gentlemen, I have nothing to say against a religion that will do this for a man. I am here to talk about a religion that is being preached by the preachers." He then went on to say that he found no fault in Christ but rather in people who did not practice what they preached.[173]

Recently, I was at a used bookstore, browsing through the section on spirituality. I found a couple of books and headed to the register. After checking out, I noticed a handwritten note stuck between the pages of a book I had purchased on the life of Christ. As I looked at the piece of paper, I was struck by its succinctness as well as its profound summary of what it means to be a follower of the Way. It simply read, "He is committed to me."

When the veil is taken away by God's grace, our awareness is expanded, our sense of his presence is heightened, and our desire to be in the light as he is in the light becomes all consuming. It is from that place of commitment that we find true rest, the inner peace all men desire but are often afraid to admit has eluded them. Our focus becomes different, our priorities change, and our compassion moves our heart for others.

Barbara Yoder records that during the nineteenth century in the Midwest, the citizens of the town of Kalamazoo gathered in prayer, wanting to see revival hover over their community. During the meeting, prayer requests were read, and one was from a woman who desired that her husband give his life to Christ.

A strong, intimidating man stood and said, "That must be me, because I have a praying wife and I know she prays for me." After asking for prayer, he sat down. Then another man stood and said, "That must be me, because I have a praying wife." All over the room, more men stood and repeated the same thing, sobbing, until 400 men had surrendered their lives to Christ.[174]

In a well-known verse of scripture often found on posters and cards, Jesus said, "Here I am! I stand at the door and knock. If anyone hears my voice and opens the door, I will come in and eat with that person, and they with me."[175] Johann Christoph Blumhardt expanded his commentary on this quote; updating the verse for contemporary audiences he wrote, "I am knocking, but you are so engrossed in your possessions, your political quarrels, and theological wrangling, that you do not hear my voice." His statement captures perfectly the climate of our day; however, he penned those words *150 years ago*. Will we be the few who learn from history so we stop repeating it?

Perhaps it is of little surprise that Las Vegas holds the distinction of being the divorce capital of the United States. A lesser-known truth about the city that claims to keep so many secrets is it is also leads the nation in suicides. It is true what they say about everything that glitters.

The challenges of our day are very real. However, Eugene Peterson captures the words of the Apostle Paul powerfully in *The Message* when he writes; "Satan's angel did his best to get me down; what he in fact did was push me to my knees."[176] It is from that posture that true victory will be obtained.

There is a particular witness in history the Amish point to when asked about an example of a person's faith that embodies what they believe is total commitment. The year was 1569 in the Netherlands, a place that at the time had a state run church. This meant that when a person was born, they were baptized as an infant among a government-approved congregation.

However, men like Dirk Willems had begun to question such forced belief systems based only on laws and not on personal decisions. His conviction was that faith was a personal choice, and baptism was something one chose to do in obedience to following Jesus, not because it was expected of everyone in the community.

Ultimately, to be baptized as an adult was considered a form of treason, seen not as an outward expression of discipleship, but rather as a public challenge to the authority of the government. As a punishment for continuing to outwardly preach the gospel and the need to be re-baptized after committing to Christ, Willems was arrested.

After being unjustly sentenced to prison, Willems escaped with the help of some friends. As he ran from the prison yard, a guard gave chase. Willems small frame allowed him to safely cross a frozen pond; the sizeable guard, however, was not so lucky. The guard plunged through the ice and into certain death. He cried out for help, and Willems went back on to the ice and pulled the man to safety.

Once on shore, the guard held Willems captive until backup arrived. Surrounding him, the soldiers questioned, "You know what we have to do to you now; why did you come back?"

Willems responded, "Jesus said to love your enemies and to do good to those who hate you. I had no other choice." Sadly, Willems was burned at the stake three days later, a picture of enduring faith and fidelity against the sharpest odds.

Years ago, I watched a movie in which the two protagonists barely defeat the bad guys. Left badly beaten on a dirt road in the middle of a desert, they will not survive much longer if they don't find the strength to crawl their way to water located miles away. They wrestle on the precipice between surrendering quietly to death and of fighting for one last breath.

The next scenes unravel quickly; first, they find a shelter that has refreshing water that revives them both physically and mentally. Then they are rescued, and their safe homecoming is celebrated. They return to their jobs, happy and healthy. Cut to a family picnic—they are with their wives and children, there is laughter and a profound sense of joy, yet there is still restlessness in the air. The men move away from the center of the party to share privacy. Their faces lose the smiles and they begin ponder, *are we really here, did this happy ending really happen, or are we still face down delirious on that dirt road dying of dehydration, simply imagining all this?*

The movie doesn't answer their question, but rather cameras pan out as the men are sitting in lawn chairs, a sense of uneasiness filling their faces.

The metaphor is profound, one we experience time and again. When life is just how we want it, we wonder when things will fall apart next. We know how transient the next new thing will be, yet we find ourselves excited when it arrives, then we are left disappointed once again after it has lost its sheen. Before long, we learn another new thing is on the horizon, and we move through the same cycle. We cry for something of substance, while holding that which is fleeting tightly in our grip.

In the midst of life, Jesus offers something permanent, a promise of his presence wherever we go, a purpose that can't be stripped away, and a vital spirituality. It comes in experiencing the promises of Christ and mixing the word of promise with an active faith.[177]

The most-used hymn from England was written in the eighteenth century by August Toplady, a former friend and colleague of John Wesley. Facing the trials of life, August would write;

Rock of Ages cleft for me
Let me hid myself in Thee;
Nothing in the hand I bring,
Simply to Thy cross I cling.

In a world made of shifting sand, where the tide of popular opinion changes from one day to the next, we need something substantial to hold onto, something that will not be moved when we lose the ground underneath our feet. In those moments, we are promised Jesus fully understands. Isaiah writes, "In all their distress he too was distressed."[178]

One night, I sat in the living room of an older couple well into their eighties. I had known them for a short while, mostly from the times they would periodically come to church. They were always quiet and withdrawn, and when they did talk, it was usually to complain. It seemed they were unhappy about nearly everything, and as the new pastor in town, I was usually their sounding board.

This night was different; the man was feeling ill, having broken a leg and feeling fearful he may not fully recover. I had stopped by to offer the assistance of the church.

"We haven't been very nice to you since you arrived," he whispered.

"Not particularly," I replied.

"You probably think all we do is criticize and grump." He mostly kept his eyes to the floor. "There is something you don't know about us." His voice began to tremble as he confessed, "Our daughter committed suicide thirty years ago. What does that say about us as parents?" He went on to share that the guilt they carried was at times unbearable.

"We should have treated you and the rest of the people better, but life can be so hard." I could tell he wanted to share more but his wife interrupted, "That is enough." He closed down, and we said our goodbyes. I gave them my cellphone number before I left, but I never heard from them again. It is true what they say in counseling: *hurt people hurt people.*

A few years ago, a friend of mine received tickets to be on a nationally televised game show. Flown out to L.A., she and her husband stood in line with other eager audience members waiting for the show to start. A producer appeared, and they were told to show enthusiasm and excitement as they waited for the doors to open, as the most exuberant guests would be invited upon stage for a chance to win money and prizes.

Unbelievably, my friend was chosen, and a staff member invited her backstage before the cameras started to roll. As she entered the room, there were several other contestants already in their seats. Then, to her great disappointment, the produces explained that the show was not as spontaneous as it appeared when televised. He then went to each person and gave them the answers to the questions they would be asked on screen and told them what prize would be theirs. Some, he explained, were to purposefully give the wrong answer and lose the game they were playing. The winners were instructed on how to act surprised when they were picked from the audience, as well as when they received their winnings. The whole thing was a charade; it was all a disappointing act.

In ancient Greece, when actors wore masks on stage for a play, the word used for them is the word from which we derive the term *hypocrite*, a term indicating someone who puts up a false front. So many people fill pews and offices across the country, putting on masks and pretending to be someone they are not, often hiding their pain from the world, afraid of what people might think if they stopped wearing a disguise. Yet Paul admonished, "Carry each other's burdens, and in this way, you will fulfill the law of Christ."[179] When we take off our masks and get honest with one another, we can help bear each other up. When people hide behind pain and then hurt others in the process, no one wins. When we confess our needs, then others can grow as they help us, and we can find healing in the midst of suffering.

When you study the life of Daniel, you learn he spent much time in prayer for his nation and for his soul. One night, he writes, "I was speaking, and praying, and confessing my sin and the sin of my people Israel, and presenting my *supplication* before the Lord my God."[180] It was then he said the angel Gabriel appeared to inform him his prayer was heard "at the beginning of thy *supplications*."[181]

In the New Testament, Paul chose this wording as he instructed people to "be anxious for nothing, but in everything by prayer and supplication"[182] present their requests to God. It is clear there is a difference between prayer and supplication, though the latter includes the former.

In the eighteenth century, Johann Leonhard Dober and David Nitschmann, two Moravian missionaries, learned of an island in the West Indies where a British atheist owned 3,000 slaves. He declared no minister would ever be allowed on the island. These two missionaries agreed to become slaves so they could live on the island and share the gospel. Their friends and families questioned such a costly decision. Seeing them off as they rowed from shore to give their lives to the men and women in slavery, Dober and Nitschmann stood up in their small vessel and proclaimed, "May the Lamb that was slain receive the reward of His suffering. May the Lamb that was slain receive the reward of His suffering!" To this day, many mission agencies use this proclamation as their own vision statement.

Daniel and Paul understood this deeper level of faith, and in their words, they give one of the secrets to accelerated growth in Christ: *supplication*. There are many types of prayer, including a short blessing before a meal, a time of giving thanks, or an offering of worship. Supplication is different; the idea contained here means to kneel before a throne and plead for one's case. Supplication is the mother in the ER desperately pleading for God to intervene and rescue her child. Supplication is the man who has lost it all, crying into his pillow and begging for heaven's hand to move. In a higher dimension, supplication is spiritual currency, what Jerry Trousdale calls "abundant prayer,"[183] which may last for hours. But supplication need not come only in a time of desperate need; it can be a moment-to-moment state of our heart as we recognize the needs around us and within us and bring them with a new and deeper authenticity in our faith before God. In fervent, believing prayer, we find it is there in supplication that we know that we have been heard.

Watchman Nee wrote that when we are confident of God's direction, "we should not then pray: 'Oh God, I ask You to do this thing.' On the contrary, we should pray: 'God, you must do this thing, it must be done this way. God, this thing must be accomplished.' This is commanding prayer—prayer of authority. The meaning of 'amen' is not 'let it be so' but 'thus shall it be.' When I say amen to your prayer I am affirming that thus shall the matter be, that what you pray shall be accomplished."[184] Or as Leonard Ravenhill put it, "God doesn't answer prayer; He answers desperate prayer!"

In 1540, Martin Luther had a dear friend named Frederick Marconis. When Frederick became sick, it was apparent his illness was terminal, leaving him only a short time to live. When Luther heard of his associate's grave condition, he wrote him a letter that read, "Frederick, I command you in Jesus' Name—you will live! You will not die because I have need of you to reform the church. The Lord will not let me hear that you are dead, but the Lord will permit you to survive me. For this I am praying. This is my will and may my will be done because I speak only to glorify the Name of God." Frederick recovered, living several more years, dying two months after Luther.[185] Such is the power of supplication.

When I was earning my degree, math was always my struggle. I had to leave two classes because the instructors made even less sense of the already difficult material. On my third attempt, I found a professor who changed everything. Before taking our first test, she simply said, "Remember, your answers have to make sense." Her simple insight helped me tremendously to go back and keep reworking problems in different manners until I reached an outcome that *made sense*. I would often have 2 or 3 different solutions to the same problem after working the numbers, but then I would pick the one that was right based on her simple, yet profound advice. When it comes to making real change, at times it is a new distinction, a word, or even just a sentence that we read or hear that clicks.

Often times, the most helpful part of change is surrounding ourselves with people who encourage our new standards and goals. Jesus talked about this principle in prayer when he said, "If two of you shall agree on earth as *touching anything* that they shall ask, it shall be done for them."[186] To *touch anything* means to make a contract of agreement with another person to work together in prayer until what is being prayed for becomes reality. As Bicket and Brandt note, "Here we have an introduction to a prayer principle of major significance. Agreement of as few as two in prayer greatly increases the effectiveness of the praying."[187] There is power when we immerse ourselves in an environment with like-minded people.

Dr. Mark Rutland shared that to overcome many painful years, he recited Psalm 23 and the Lord's Prayer dozens of times per day, a practice he still continues.[188] For Jim Marion, writing proved cathartic in releasing toxic emotions. Through the pen, he found healing from anger because, "Underneath depression, there is always anger; under the anger, there is always fear; and under the fear, there is always hurt."[189] Honestly encountering these dark shadows through journaling has brought freedom to countless individuals. Others have found renewal in silent retreats. Still, some were made whole by just knowing another person cared they existed. Sometimes more conventional counseling or coaching helps remove subconscious blocks so we see more clearly. Paul would also warn that the enemy of our souls works hard to keep us blind so we need to regularly pray for spiritual eyesight.[190]

It may be one or many of these principles that help us to finally make the shift. When Hernando Cortes led a group of men into Mexico to conquer the Aztecs and find their massive treasure, he had 11 ships and several hundred men. Once the ships touched land, he ordered them burned, forcefully telling the men there was no going back. Once he made a commitment, he eliminated any other alternatives. That was total dedication, an essential component of moving to a different level of living.

Penitentiaries were precursors to modern-day prisons. There was a time when criminals would be placed in a cell to do penance, that is to stay until one experienced profound regret for their crimes. Once a person reached this point, they would be set free. Perhaps this would happen in a few months, or maybe in a few years, but the goal was to come to a place of inner change by seeing things more clearly.

Philippa Perry writes of the labs of psychoanalysis Carl Jung's mentees, where "there was also a little cell called an oratorium. Here, they prayed for and meditated upon a successful outcome. And, true to the orthodoxies of their day, written above the door to the little oratorium were the words 'Deo concedente' – God willing.'"[191] It was an understanding that our ultimate healing comes with help from above.

In the nineteenth century, a famous contest was proposed. Atheist Charles Bradlaugh challenged Hugh Price Hughes to publically debate the question of God's existence. At the time, Hughes served in some of London's most poverty-stricken slums.

The idea of these two well-respected men sharing opposite sides of the argument concerning man's greatest question caught the attention of the city. Boastful, Bradlaugh was sure of the victory.

Hughes agreed to the debate, on one condition. "I propose to you that we each bring some concrete evidences of the validity of our beliefs in the form of men and women who have been redeemed from the lives of sin and shame by the influence of our teaching. I will bring 100 such men and women, and I challenge you to do the same."

Hughes then said if Bradlaugh could not find 100 changed lives, then he could bring just 50 people. If he could not find 50, then 20 would suffice, or even just ten. He finally ended, "Nay, Mr. Bradlaugh, I challenge you to bring one, just one man or woman who will make such a testimony regarding the uplifting of your atheistic teachings." It was then that Bradlaugh withdrew from the debate.

David would sing, "My help comes from the LORD, the Maker of heaven and earth."[192] In the end, he will help us to rise up, to face the challenges, to find strength for the day, and to be more than we could ever dream, because after all, it is he who makes us well.

CHAPTER 5

SOMETHING TO BELIEVE IN

"Be nice. Until it's time to not be nice."[193]

– **James Dalton** (Patrick Swayze), *Road House* (1989)

Elisabeth Kübler-Ross probably spent more time with people who were dying than anyone else in history. I listened as she was asked during an interview if there was any advice that people at the end of their lives offered. She didn't hesitate with her answer.

Ross did not see herself becoming a psychiatrist to the dying, but in a time of need during the Second World War, she stepped into the role for a community of people in desperate need of compassion. She would learn much from her patients, and she later suggested her research benefited all people, as death is not only when a person's heart stops beating, but it can include such things as the end of a season of life or a relationship. She passed on her research in the form of what are now the familiar stages of grief. The stages can also be applied broadly to major life events, such as a divorce, the end of a career, or an unsettling diagnosis from a doctor.

The first stage is denial: *this can't be happening to me*. This is often followed by anger, *why me?* Perhaps bargaining is the most interesting. At this third stage people make a deal with God, promising to get involved in charity work, change their ways, and attend worship more faithfully, if only he would answer their prayer. (Ross would go on to say that when the crisis was over, few if any kept these commitments.) The final stages are depression and then acceptance of the diagnosis.

When the interviewer asked for the most important lesson the dying taught her, Ross quickly responded in only four words, "Leave no unfinished business."[194]

If you want to learn to dance, then learn to dance. If you want to compose a masterpiece, begin today. Want to learn a foreign language or travel to an exotic land? Begin making steps towards that goal before the sun sets tonight. If you need to make an apology, don't wait. If there is someone you need to talk to, make the call or write the letter.

This is why the oft-told story of William Borden inspires so many people to being *now*. A wealthy heir, Borden travelled the world before college and saw untold suffering. His heart was moved to join the mission field. To solidify his commitment, in his Bible he wrote: *No Reserves*. His family encouraged him to finish college before making a final decision on a career. Upon graduation, he was still determined to alleviate the pain he witnessed overseas, feeling a special calling to go to China. He then wrote two more words in his Bible: *No Retreats*. After saying his goodbyes, he set sail for the Far East. The ship stopped in Egypt where Borden became ill. He died four weeks later.

His story is not told as a cautionary tale about the price of sacrifice, but rather as an encouragement to leave no unfinished business. His final words are an enduring call to move into your destiny. Before he died, Borden wrote two more words in his Bible. Underneath *No Reserves, No Retreats,* he wrote, *No Regrets.*

How do you live a life with no regrets? The word *decision* means "to cut off." When a person makes a decision where they will not stand for things to continue as they have been, they are cutting off the alternative of going backwards. As Michael Jeffreys notes, "Your whole life changes the day you make the decision you will no longer settle for mediocrity."[195] It may mean leaving a job, getting counseling, waking up early, signing up for the gym, but in the end, it requires taking responsibility. A century ago G. H. Lewes advised, "The only cure for grief is action." Movement is what makes the difference.

We all know people who talk about making a change, or being a different person, but never follow through. Someone once told me you can block out the sun with a dime. If you hold a coin close enough to your eye, you will not be able to see anything else, no matter how massive it is. In life, we can easily miss the bigger picture for the smallest of reasons. For many it is unexamined beliefs, such as *I am told old* or *too young, I will start tomorrow, It is no big deal, No one cares, I've tried in the past and nothing changed.* We can always find a reason to play it safe; as previously noted, this is partially because our brain is adverse to risk, which is part of its survival mechanism. In turn, it readily supplies enough emotions and thoughts to keep us from leaving our comfort zone. This is one reason powerful events like a fire-walk make such a difference. When you do what you don't think you can do, you expand what you believe is possible with every limitation you surpass. Then incredible things begin to happen as you overcome the brain's imagined limitations by doing something you imagine is impossible, like walking on hot coals.

But you are not your thoughts, you are not your brain. You have to take conscious control of your mind and overcome the excuses with powerful reasons to move forward; otherwise, you are in danger of ending your life filled with regret and unfinished business. As an anonymous writer penned, "To live is to risk dying. To hope is to risk despair. To try is to risk failure. But risks must be taken because the greatest hazard in life is to risk nothing. The person who risks nothing, does nothing, has nothing and is nothing. They may avoid suffering and sorrow, but they cannot learn, feel, change, grow, love, live. Chained by their certitudes, they are as a slave, they have forfeited their freedom. Only a person who risks is free."[196]

During a message to his disciples, Jesus said, "Occupy till I come."[197] The wording here indicates improving something. It has been well said that our lives are either a warning or an example. To be the latter, we need to leave things better than we find them, including the lives of people we influence.

I once listened as a coach gave someone advice about issues they were facing. He said that while we all have problems, we need to get rid of the *boring ones*. It is far too easy to be consumed with boring problems: dealing with rude people that we allow to ruin our day, getting worked up over small things, allowing our emotions to be manipulated by fear tactics in the media and arguing over nonsense.

In *The Source New Testament* translation by A. Nyland, she notes that the word for *hypocrite*, one who wears a mask like a stage actor and lives their life covering up who they really are, should more readily be translated as *hypercritical*. Thus, she translates Jesus' message as words of warning to avoid being like the "overly critical, hair splitting, pedantic religious people."[198] It seems there are few things that bring out the pettiness in people as much as religious preferences.

As the old joke goes, "How many church members does it take to change a light bulb?"

"Change? My grandmother donated that light bulb!"

Moving past boring, hypercritical arguments, we need to learn to consider more deeply how we can occupy and improve the things around us.

Before David would face Goliath, he first approached his brothers to ask them why the other soldiers were letting the giant taunt the army of Israel. His brothers were angry at his boldness, feeling he was insulting them for being cowards. They demanded he leave the battlefield and return home. David responded, "Is there not a cause?"[199]

David's words are a powerful declaration of a different quality of life. What he was asking was simply, is there not more at stake than one another's egos, is there not something more important than our own comfort, is there not something bigger than our own lives to live for?

In short, he was expressing the principle of finding a big enough *why* to take action. As John Fuhrman states, "*Why* we do something most often determines the outcome. Average people have often lost their reason *why*."[200]

A long time ago, I gave up interest in debating with *overly critical, hair splitting, pedantic religious people*. There are times to move on and stop being nice and to quit going along to get along. Each of us has to decide on a bigger "why" for our decisions; otherwise, we will simply cave to the pressures of public opinion and give up. For David, the "why" was the reputation of his nation and his God. Shortly after this statement, he went into the valley and defeated Goliath.

When you and I look out over the communities in which we live, when we are moved from our comfort zone and want to make a change, there must be a big enough *why* to fuel us forward to face the giants standing between us and our destiny. Find a big enough why, and you will find a way to breakthrough. As Jim Rohn would often say, "Reasons come first, answers second."

Most people have little motivation to work for a paycheck. They may come to work, but they will not be fully present, nor will they give their best. Study after study shows money is not near the motivator people believe it is. There is nothing wrong with working at a job you don't like. But beyond using your money to pay for bills, what happens inside when instead you realize you can use your paycheck to bring freedom to a hurting life, food to a hungry child, or a gift to a broken-hearted friend? Suddenly, you are on your way to finding big enough reasons to put in the extra work as you expand your vision. Perhaps your heart is moved by the horror of the following statistics: *twenty-seven million* people around the world are trafficked in slavery, half of which are children.[201] Suddenly, you realize that part of the paycheck can be used to bring light to such darkness, and now you are finding a big enough *why*. As Ademola shares, "Every dollar that God gives you has a divine assignment attached to it."[202]

The first day of a new year will never provide enough inspiration to push you towards making lasting changes. But when you examine where you are, and what you dream that life could be while imagining all the people you could impact along the way, the richness of that picture will help propel you forward day to day to give more of yourself.

When my wife and I first thought about buying a house, *we took a walk*. At the time, we were living in a rundown apartment with a leaky ceiling and a broken air conditioner. Repair requests after repair requests were ignored by the landlord. So, we took a walk, and then another, and another.

We would drive to a nice neighborhood, park on the street, and walk down the sidewalks admiring the houses. We would look at the smiling faces of families as we passed them by, listening to their laughter as they cooked out in their yards. Others were sitting in folding chairs enjoying the peaceful quiet of a cool, breezy night.

Our apartment was in a bad neighborhood, with lots of noise, and too much crime. Family did not feel safe visiting after it got dark. But on these walks, we expanded our vision, we felt the dream in our hearts, and we pictured what it would be like to take a stroll each night without being concerned about potential muggers. We could literally feel the warmth of our new fireplace, and smell the hot chocolate being shared with loved ones gathered around the fire.

Within six months of that first walk, we were homeowners in a house just like the one we pictured in our minds. First, we felt deep in our hearts the reasons *why* we needed to move, and when that feeling rose from deep inside our core, we moved towards and reached our goal.

Mark Batterson states, "I believe we are all one prayer away from a totally different life."[203] When we seek to see the world from a different place, from a perspective of love and sacrifice and possibility, things can begin to rapidly shift as our priorities begin to reshuffle.

Perhaps you want to be a better husband or a better father. Ask yourself why you want that. Is it simply to meet your own needs, to bring a sense of security to your own life? Is it because you want to be happy or to have a good public image? While reasons such as these are not necessarily right or wrong, they are limiting because they only revolve around what you want, and the consequence of focusing only on ourselves is that life gets boring very fast.

What if you had bigger reasons? Maybe you want to be a better husband because you love to see your wife smile, or because she deserves a man who will put his fear on the shelf and learn to love her fully. Maybe it is because you take seriously the words of Paul who says your reason for living is to die for her,[204] and the warrior inside you is drawn to such a challenge.

Do you want to lose weight? Why? Is it simply to lose a few pounds, or because other people at the office are doing it? You will not likely succeed with such low level reasons. Perhaps, on the other hand, you want to serve others, and you know that only with vibrant energy will you be able to give completely to them, so you want to be your fittest. Or maybe you know the long-term risks of the increased possibility of disease, and you want to know that even though your birthday candles may change each year, you don't have to get older because you can maintain the vibrant health and glow from your youth because you treat your body like a temple.

Some other ways to come up with a bigger *why* are to stop and ask yourself what important lessons you have learned in the past year, what problem you have most benefitted from, and what have you most needed to relearn. Then consider what suffering you see around you that moves your heart, and reflect on ways you can most effectively help.

I was listening to Darren Hardy speak, and he said something that stuck with me as I quickly scribbled it down, "Commitment is doing the thing you said you were going to do long after the mood you said it in has left you."

Car dealers and realtors know the average sale happens within 48 hours of a customer expressing interest. If time goes beyond that, buyers are far less likely to make a purchase. Commitments come and go for many people, often made on a whim.

How much better to know someone with integrity who does the right thing simply because they said they would. Many of us know people who are constantly trying to pass off some opportunity if only we would give them money.

One of those moments recently arrived in my life as a man knew my desire to reach others through teaching, writing and coaching. He was trying to sell me the moon if I would partner with him, only he was having a cash-flow problem. Though his offer was appealing, I decided to wait and see if he had character that could be trusted. My initial gut reaction was that he was simply a smooth talker. Solomon cautioned, "Do not let your mouth lead you into sin."[205]

It wasn't long before I learned I was correct about this person, as a few months later, he was accused of extreme perversion, caught in numerous lies throughout the community, and eventually went into hiding. He sank into depression and shortly thereafter died of a heart attack due to the pressure and charges surrounding him. Billy Graham stated, "When character is lost, all is lost." Unfortunately, there are countless smallminded people looking to make gains at the expense of others without having done the hard work of conforming their inner self to reflect an elevated standard.

One of the biggest myths sold in our culture is *you can't take it with you*. This is simply not true. People often die with dreams still in their heart. Worse are the ones who take their bitterness to the grave, failing to make amends. I can assure you that many angry people stay angry on their deathbed, depressed people stay depressed, and bitter people stay bitter. The romantic idea of reconciling with someone in their final moments after they have spent decades harboring hurts is mostly a Hollywood fantasy. If you think the time is going to come that a person will magically change simply because they are older or are facing death, you are most likely mistaken. I have officiated funerals where police officers were required to be present, such was the hatred between family members. You have to be conscious to make a change. This is why Paul prayed that "the eyes of your heart may be enlightened."[206] Most people are asleep and don't even know it. This is why the time to change is now when you can see things more clearly.

One day, I was called to the hospital by family I did not know. At the time, I was a pastor in the area and was asked to come see a man who was dying. He had been given hours to live as his kidneys were failing. When I came into the room, his three daughters were standing around his bed, and it was clear I had interrupted an argument. The father had turned away from all three of them, so I approached the side of the bed he was facing.

I had no longer introduced myself, when he began to tell me how disappointed he had always been in his children, and how angry he was at a corrupt business man who had essentially stole his money. I attempted to change his focus, but he simply repeated again what he had previously said. I told him I was sorry that his health was failing, and that I understood that the situation looked impossible, but I believed God could do anything. I explained that the hospital had asked me to stop and pray with him, as there was always hope.

An intern appeared at the door and said they needed to immediately take him for further testing on a different floor. I watched as the daughters tried to tell him they would be waiting in the lobby, but he refused to look at them. I said a short prayer with him before he was wheeled away, and I could tell his daughters were fighting to hold back tears of anger and regret.

When he was gone, I asked the sisters what had happened. With fury in their faces, they shared that their dad had told them he never cared for any of them, and that he was leaving his entire inheritance to their brother. They left the room arguing with each other, catching glares from several people in the lobby. I inquired with the hospital a few days later, and the man had indeed died.

Another time I had recently arrived at a church where a shrill, old woman named Edith frightened the children, the adults, and several of the former pastors away. Many were convinced she practiced dark magic. When we first met, she told me it wouldn't take long before I would find out who was really in charge. Within two months, I fired her nephew who openly threw tantrums on staff. Edith quickly realized her days of bullying were at an end. For months, she mailed me nasty letters and left strange voicemails—all tactics that had apparently worked in the past to scare previous pastors out of town. Like all bullies, until someone stands up to them, they will continue to run over others unabashed.

Finally, one day, a man I had never seen before stopped by my office. When he introduced himself I was little surprised, "I am Edith's son, but you have probably never heard of me."

"I have not," I told him. Edith had previously only mentioned having daughters. However, somehow I had assumed something like this would happen.

He continued, "Over *twenty-five* years ago, she disowned me when I got kicked out of school. She said I embarrassed her, and I was no longer her son. She hasn't talked to me since." Intrigued,

I explained that I had witnessed her at her worst and could appreciate his predicament.

As he stood to leave, he finished, "I have tried for two decades to contact her, but she is filled with hate like no other and refuses all my attempts. If she treats her own flesh and blood like that, you never stood a chance."

"I know," I assured him. He got in his car, drove away and never returned.

In Rome, when an army's victory was publicly celebrated, an aide would walk behind the soldiers in the parade and whisper, *Memento mori*, a Latin phrase that means, "Remember you are mortal and will die."[207] It was a reminder that tomorrow is not promised to anyone, and that now is the time to embrace life and live with passion.

I cannot stress highly enough, today is the day to pray for open eyes. We have to be deliberate in examining ourselves. This is why it is so critical to pay attention to your thinking and habitual patterns.

Most of us learn far too little from history, even from our own ancestry. Few people know much about their grandparents, let alone their great-grandparents. You would be surprised how angry and depressed some of the men from these older generations truly are, regardless of the idealistic picture we all want to hold.

Perhaps the unrest and the dysfunction some of these men leave behind has something to do with studies that reveal that during World War II, the average American soldier cheated on his wife with 25 different women and prostitutes. Unfortunately, the numbers during the Vietnam War remained the same,[208] which among other factors, has contributed to the sad fact that over 90% of Vietnam vets are divorced.[209]

In the early twentieth century, things took a dark turn when by 1935, some 35 states "enacted laws requiring the sexual isolation and sterilization of 'unfit people' including...the 'feeble-minded,' chronic criminals and even epileptics."[210] Roughly 70,000 Americans were sterilized against their will before the practice was banned.

What baggage have our ancestors been hiding? What poison did previous generations pass down, perhaps of things even in our own family of which we are unaware? As Johnson notes, "An excellent Minirth/Meier book entitled *Kids Who Carry Our Pain* accurately states that our children deal with and finish the pain that we didn't work through in our own lives. But I take that one step further: Kids not only carry our pain, *they also carry the consequences of our sin.*"[211]

Ask most men if they have been close to their fathers, and they will give you a blank stare. (It is generally accepted that most people derive their image of God from their fathers, which is another reason it is critical for men to begin taking this role more seriously.) What damage do families continue to relive when relationship wounds are left unaddressed for years on end, and old patterns just keep repeating with new faces? It is time to break these cycles of destruction.

At his trial, Jesus told Pilate that those who seek the truth will listen to his words. Pilate famously responded, "What is truth?"[212] By this time, Pilate had been through countless conflicts and had known man broken trusts, some from his own doing, and others from politicians who sought to destroy him. Cynicism and exhaustion had set in, and though he was standing next to the Messiah, he found it hard to believe real answers or hope existed.

The prophet Zechariah told the people, "Do not despise the day of small beginnings."²¹³ The people of his day faced the daunting task of rebuilding a city amidst their enemies. They were ready to give up the reconstruction. Zechariah encouraged the people to understand that any step in the right direction, no matter how small, was progress. Happiness is found when progress is made. Relationships can be mended one word at a time.

It is said that Walt Disney was told a mouse on a huge movie screen would frighten women and children, yet because he took action, moved beyond the critics, and followed simple steps forward, today, Mickey Mouse is one of the most recognizable characters in the entire world.²¹⁴ Today is the day of a new beginning if we can believe it and see things differently than other people.

Years ago, an unknown author wrote a story about the day the devil was selling his possessions. For those willing to pay the price, it was an opportunity to buy equipment from the prince of darkness.

When he opened the doors, crowds poured in to look at each item. There were the famous tools of his trade; envy, lust, hate, greed, gossip, and all the rest. Each was displayed attractively, and each had a price tag attached.

However, one odd-looking tool had a note tied to it that read, "Not for sale." Finally, curious onlookers asked, "What is that tool over there?"

The devil replied, "That is discouragement."

"Why is it not for sale?" the people asked. The evil one explained, "Because it is the most useful tool of all. I can reach a man with that tool when all other tools fail to work. Once I get inside his mind with that, I can manipulate him in many ways. You will notice it is well worn. That is because I use it often." To this day, the tool has never been sold, and the devil takes every opportunity to use it on men and women everywhere.

Discouragement often stops people from trying, whether it is to heal a relationship or move towards a goal. The enemy often whispers, "For you, things will never change." Don't let opposition stop you. One thing to do when you are discouraged is to realize that adversity is often where our strength grows. In fact, in the early church the disciples celebrated when they were *arrested*. On one occasion they were whipped by the authorities. Afterwards Luke notes, "The apostles left the Sanhedrin, rejoicing because they had been counted worthy of suffering disgrace for the Name."[215]

Why would they rejoice? At least two reasons. One, they counted it an honor when they faced opposition because they believed it was an indication they must be doing something right. As Jean De La Bruyere said, "Out of difficulties grow miracles." The second reason is they realized that it was in the stressful times their faith would grow the most. They knew they would expand their faith further after a few days facing the confines of imprisonment than they would experience after months of easy living. Shalom Arush notes that "coping with adversity elevates a person. Without difficulties and challenges it's very hard for a person to grow, since by nature we all want everything to go smoothly in life, and to take it easy...Throughout all generations the greatest people have been the ones who stood up and to, and conquered, adversity."[216]

This doesn't mean hard times feel good, or we should seek them out. What it does do is give us a deeper understanding that pain can lead to growth, so instead of running from it, we can stop and observe it and uncover the greater lessons found in it. As Ray Dalio shares, "There is nothing to prompt learning like pain and necessity."[217]

Personally, there were times in the past when I would speak at a funeral, and people would question if I could identify with their pain. Now however, at this time in my life, I have lost many of those closest to me, and no one questions any longer if I understand the valley of the shadow of death. Believe me, I would give anything to have the ones I love back in my life, but we have to deal with what is in front of us, not dwell on things we cannot change. I know some people give up when life comes crashing down. I can promise you it is far better to learn from those moments and build spiritual muscle so you can give your strength to others in their time of need. As James Malinchak states, "Adversity can be your best university." Our job is the find the lessons to be learned.

John Newton, creator of "Amazing Grace," shared, "We will look back upon the experiences through which the Lord led us and be overwhelmed by adoration and love for him. We will then see and acknowledge that mercy and goodness directed every step. We shall see that what we once mistakenly called afflictions and misfortunes were in reality blessings without which we would not have grown in faith."

It is important to highlight that when other people get uncomfortable with our growth, we need to recognize this can be a signal that we are making progress. You may get a promotion or lose weight and find that people you thought were close friends will not celebrate with you. Don't get discouraged, and realize they may be threatened by your positive changes. It is not because they are unhappy about your success; but rather your moving forward reminds them they are not. As John L. Mason states, "Ingratitude and criticism are going to come; they are a part of the price paid for leaping past mediocrity."[218]

In 1846, Ignaz Semmelweis made the initial observation that if surgeons washed their hands between procedures, patients stopped getting ill after surgery. He began to demand his staff wash their hands before and after seeing a patient. However, other medical professionals did not agree with Semmelweis. He was mocked for his theories, and eventually placed in a mental institution where he died.

There will always be critics, but don't let them stop your forward movement. Today countless lives have been spared because Semmelweis understood the absolute necessity of hygiene and refused to surrender to peer pressure or majority opinion.

There is an ancient story in the Book of Kings about four lepers during a time of famine. Leprosy automatically made a person an outcast that was required to isolate themselves from society and live outside the city gates. It was common for someone with this disease to sort through the trash looking for food, or be forced to beg from strangers. If someone did come near them unknowingly the leper was to shout a warning saying, "Unclean! Unclean!"

It is not hard to imagine the pain, brokenness and loneliness of such a situation. People with the same condition would naturally gravitate towards one another. These four men had been travelling together for some time, watching each other's backs, shunned by society. However, famine was ravaging the land and they were starving. They reasoned, "Why stay here until we die?"[219]

Close by, they knew an enemy army was positioned, so they decided to roll the dice and hope to find mercy and food there. When they reached the camp, they found it had been abandoned overnight, the soldiers having fled upon hearing loud noises from heaven. The lepers waded through the camp and found food, a fresh change of clothes, and vast deposits of silver and gold. After they had their share, they felt guilty, knowing other people were starving as well. They went and told their kinsmen what they found, and the story ends with all the people taking their fill and having a great celebration.[220]

Someone has said that the gospel is one hungry person showing another hungry person where to find food. Like the lepers, we have all felt like outsiders, and we have all known betrayal and loss. When our eyes are open and we see truth more clearly, it is like a fresh meal and a change of clothes. It is like uncovering gold. Everything changes when we understand God's "immortality program."[221]

As A. B. Simpson said over a century ago, "The gospel tells rebellious men that to God they are reconciled, that justice is satisfied, that sin has been atoned for, that the judgment of the guilty may be revoked, the condemnation of the sinner canceled, the curse of the Law blotted out, the gates of hell closed, the portals of heaven opened wide, the power of sin subdued, the guilty conscience healed, the broken heart comforted, and the sorrow and misery of the Fall undone."

Our task though is not to keep such wisdom to ourselves, but rather by word and deed share it with other people so they can leave their own famines and shackles behind. That is one of the secrets of life, giving to others what we have received and to see them light up when their eyes are opened.

Nine centuries ago, Bernard of Clairvaux wrote, "There are many who seek knowledge for the sake of knowledge: that is curiosity. There are others who desire to know in order that they may be known: that is vanity. But there are those who seek knowledge in order to edify others: that is love."

At the Harold Church in Staunton, England, there is an inscription that reads, "In the year of 1653, when all things sacred were throughout the nation destroyed or profaned, this church was built to the glory of God by Sir Robert Shirley, whose singular praise it was to have done the best things in the worst times."

What a legacy, to have done the *best things in the worst times*. First we make our choices, then our choices make us. Let us choose wisely; *is there not a cause?*

CHAPTER 6

GRACE IS GREATER

"There is enough grace in God's heart of love to save and keep saved for time and eternity, every sinner that ever has or ever will live, and then enough left over to save a million more universes full of sinners, were there such, and then some more."

– **Kenneth S. Wuest**

George Grenfell felt called to be a missionary in the Congo, at the time known as "the shortcut to Heaven," due in part to local headhunters, cannibals and witch doctors. His dream was to bring a ship down the river and evangelize tribes deep in the jungle. It was the late nineteenth century, and boats had not successfully pierced the waterways in this part of Africa. Though he would bury his wife and children during his time in the Congo, Grenfell knew his heart was in the right place.

In 1877, a wealthy benefactor donated a boat to his dream. The daunting task was how to get the ship to Africa. To move the boat from England to the Congo River required taking it apart and shipping it in 800 boxes to the river's mouth. The three engineers who were to organize the ship's reconstruction all died within weeks of arriving on site, leaving the task to Grenfell. Miraculously, the ship was pieced back together and would go on to travel over a thousand miles on its initial voyage, reaching tribes once deemed unreachable.

In 1886, Grenfell received a gold medal from the Royal Geographic Society. He died in 1906, having touched many lives. His last words were, "Jesus is mine."[222] Incredible, almost unbelievable things happen when someone decides to move from talking about it to doing the work.

In the United States, most heart attacks happen on Monday mornings. Research shows that one-fourth of employees view their jobs as the number one stressor in their lives, while forty-three percent of employees often feel anger toward their employers as a result of feeling overworked and underappreciated.[223] We need a greater sense of mission and passion to compel us forward.

Recently, my wife and I were enjoying the slower rhythm of life in Amish county. We stopped and visited some farms, took a buggy ride, and chatted with the locals at the market. As we headed down the road to find something to eat, we passed a painted sign that read, "Used books for sale." I have often found some of the most interesting books in stores found off the beaten path. Inside a barn, there were tables where passersby had left books for other travelers. With no one else around, I browsed until I found a few titles that caught my attention, then left a five-dollar bill in the bucket marked, "Honor system." I had picked up a dusty old copy of a hardcover on prayer by Cecil Murphey. As I spent the next two days devouring the words, I was especially drawn to his suggestion for the weary wanderer looking to recapture the luster of life. There, Murphey taught the sojourner to pray daily, "Lord, I need to grow. Make me want to grow."[224] To recapture wonder is critical in life.

I remember watching in amazement as Michael Flatley set a world record by tap dancing an astounding 28 taps in one *second*. To an interviewer who told him that was impossible, Flatley just smiled and said, "You have to believe."

As a photographer, I enjoy taking fast-action shots of nature. A hummingbird beats its wings some 70 times per second, so capturing an image of one of these small birds with its wings frozen in midair is particularly challenging. However, its speed pales in comparison to a true wonder: the tiny mosquito, whose wings beat an astonishing 600 times *per second*!

Some things are simply hard to believe. One of those things in particular is the idea of *grace*. At its core, the word itself is where we get the term *gift*. It is counterintuitive to accept the value of forgiveness along with the concept of receiving it for free. We are used to earning approval, often working hard to gain the slightest amount. Many people live with a scarcity mindset that somehow there is not enough love to go around, so they retain their affections, afraid to risk giving them away. The irony is that holding on to love instead of giving it away is the very reason individuals don't experience more of it in the first place. As John Gray writes, "The greatest emotional pain we can experience in life occurs when we stop sharing our love with the people we love the most."[225]

Grace, expressed most fully when Christ rose triumphantly from the grave, means there is nothing we can do to make God love us more, and there is nothing we can do that would cause him to love us less.

Years ago, an unknown author shared the story about a former prostitute who gave her life to Christ. She eventually fell in love with the minister's son and they got engaged. Because of her scandalous past, people questioned the wisdom of such a unity. As the people began to debate whether the couple should be married, the woman began to cry. Incensed, her husband-to-be stood and said, "My fiancée's past is not what is on trial here. What you are questioning is the ability of the blood of Jesus to wash away sin. Today, you have put the blood of Jesus on trial. So, does it wash away sin or not?"[226] The congregation began to weep as they realized the wisdom of his words.

In the fourth century, Ambrose of Milan wrote, "Jesus, I wish you would let me wash your feet, since it was by walking about in me that you soiled them. I wish you would give me the task of wiping the stains from your feet, since it was my behavior that put them there. But where can I get the running water I need to wash your feet? If I have no water, at least I have tears. Let me wash your feet with my tears, and wash myself at the same time."[227] Here was one deeply in touch with the need for the power of mercy.

It has been well said that if you want to experience scarcity in your life, then begin to play fair. The temptation is always there before us to give what we get, to keep track of who owes us, and to get even when the opportunity arises. When someone is rude on the highway, we often return the favor. When we feel that justice has fallen short, something inside us feels determined to balance the scales, no matter the cost. If a spouse says a cutting comment, we return one. If another person withholds love, we do the same. We are all experts at playing fair.

When Jesus rose, he shifted long-held beliefs about right and wrong. Though his close friend had turned his back in his hour of need, Jesus had not done the same. At the tomb, the angel instructed Mary to "tell his disciples *and Peter*"[228] that Jesus was alive. There was a special emphasis made to go and find Jesus' friend who was in hiding, ashamed of running away during the trial of Christ, and to tell him of the forgiveness and grace being poured out by the Son.

When David Livingstone first set sail to Africa, worried family and friends followed him to the port before he boarded his ship. Concerned for his safety, they reminded him of the dangers of Africa, including meeting unknown tribes, as well as encountering wild animals and mysterious diseases. One young man was especially adamant that he remain in England.

Opening his Bible to the book of Matthew, Livingstone read the words of Christ, "Lo, I am with you always." He closed the book, turned to the young man and smiled and said, "That, my friend, is the word of a gentleman...So let us be going."[229]

At the forefront of the countless promises men have been offered in Christ is the need to receive and understand the power of forgiveness and grace. Though it may seem impossible such love exists, we are called to simply believe. It is to this end that John Newton, the redeemed slave trader and author of "Amazing Grace," shared at the end of his life, "Although my memory's fading, I remember two things very clearly: I am a great sinner and Christ is a great Savior."

For centuries, men have tried to run a mile in four minutes. It was attempted for thousands of years. The Romans and Greeks even tied athletes to bulls so they would run faster as they developed stronger leg muscles, but in the end, no one was able to complete the mile in four minutes. It was simply deemed that the physiological makeup of human beings prohibited them from this feat.

However, in a well-known slice of history, one man shattered millennia of belief when he did in fact run the mile in four minutes in 1954. Roger Bannister finally did what people had tried to do for thousands of years, giving people a new reference about what was possible.

Amazingly, once people had a new belief because of his model, within the next twelve months, some two dozen others were able to break the four minute mile as well—something that today is a common occurrence. It is remarkable how everything changes when the truth is uncovered and lies fade away.

Consider the compelling case of the man known simply as Mr. Wright. A patient of Dr. Klopfer, he was diagnosed with a very aggressive cancer, and there came a time when he wasn't expected to live through the night. Tumors riddled his body and his lungs were barely operating, leaving him dependent upon an oxygen mask.

All that changed when Mr. Wright heard about a new drug called Krebiozen, a possible miracle cure. Though Dr. Klopfer saw little point in administering the drug, he gave the allotted dose to Wright and then went home for the weekend, certain it would be the last time he saw his dying patient. However, when he returned Monday morning, the unbelievable had happened: Wright had almost fully recovered.

Though the other patients on the drug had not shown signs of improvement, Wright rapidly improved and was sent home ten days later in perfect health. Two months later, the FDA reported that Krebiozen was ineffective in treating cancer. Upon hearing this report, Wright became ill once again, and bizarrely, his tumors returned, requiring that he be readmitted to the hospital.

By now, Dr. Klopfer realized that belief was playing a major role in his patient's health. Wanting to test the placebo effect, he told Wright about another drug that he knew would work.

Eagerly, Wright agreed to the treatment, not realizing he was simply receiving an injection of sterilized water.

Again, Wright rapidly improved and his tumors disappeared, and once again, he was sent home. Ironically, it would be another news report, again about the worthlessness of Krebiozen that would send Wright back to the hospital a third and final time. He died two days later. Andrew Newberg notes that in a report in the *Journal of Projective Techniques*, it was recorded, "Dr. Klopfer concluded that when the power of Wright's optimistic beliefs expired, his resistance to the disease expired as well."[230]

How powerful beliefs truly are. They can serve us or hinder us. Dietrich Bonhoeffer once stated, "Satan does not fill us with hatred of God but with forgetfulness of God."[231] So many things cloud up our thinking, crowding out right beliefs and replacing them with subtle distractions, which is why it is imperative that our values be based upon the truth as revealed in Jesus Christ.

The Apostle Paul wrote, "God has bound *all* men over to disobedience so that he may have mercy on them *all*."[232] Even our sin is used by God to lead us back to him. When a person dwells in the darkness it serves its purpose of showing them how empty it truly is so they can then be directed back to the source of light.

Many people know what it is like to come to a place where they can identify with Solomon's statement that pursuing so many empty promises is just like *chasing the wind*. That is why grace is so amazing, because we don't have to seek it, and we can't try to earn it; it is something we simply receive.

In 1921, David and Svea Flood went to the Congo as missionaries. They were accompanied by their baby and another couple. Unable to get close to a certain tribe, they made a home a short distance away. Eventually, the other couple gave up and left, while David and Svea stayed behind to try and befriend the locals.

The village chief allowed only one young boy to visit the home of the missionaries to sell them food. The couple took each opportunity to tell this boy about the risen Christ. Tragically, Svea died just days after giving birth to her second child.

David became consumed by bitterness, and shortly thereafter, he left the mission field with his son, leaving the newborn baby girl at the missionary station with some friends. Sadly, this couple too died. The baby, Aina, was adopted by an American couple who moved back to the States.

Aggie, as she became known, grew up with a wonderful new family, eventually marrying and having children of her own. Her husband became president of a college in Seattle, and Aggie eventually began to search for her ancestry. One day, while perusing a magazine, she saw a picture with a grave marked, "Svea Flood."

The article accompanying the photo shared about the tragic story of her parents. However, it continued by discussing the life of the young boy who sold food to the Flood family. When David had left, the young boy in the village shared the gospel message with the tribe and 600 people became believers.

Aggie became determined to find her father and tell him how the story had ended. When she did locate him, he was very ill, having long ago become an alcoholic. When they finally came face-to-face, he immediately recognized her and wept, sorry he had not taken her with him when she was only a baby.

She eagerly told him that his efforts had made a tremendous impact on the village, and that her mother's death had not been in vain, but rather had transformed hundreds of lives. After years of bitterness and pain, David finally returned to his faith in God, dying shortly after he was reunited with his daughter.

Aggie eventually traveled to Africa to meet the boy who sold food to her parents. Now a grown man, she learned he had a ministry that was impacting over 100,000 people in churches and schools across the nation.[233]

In *The Message Paraphrase* by Eugene Peterson, he translates the words of Jesus, "Are you tired? Worn out? Burned out on religion? Come to me. Get away with me and you'll recover your life. Walk with me and work with me—watch how I do it. Learn the unforced rhythms of grace...Keep company with me and you'll learn to live freely and lightly."[234]

How different it is to know the truth that we don't have to perform, but that we can instead rest in the love of God that is already ours. We can know Jesus understands our fear and pain and of the hopelessness of religions that are filled with reward and punishment and empty answers. Instead, how liberating when our hearts are truly able to "grasp how wide and long and high and deep is the love of Christ."[235]

Eternity magazine counted six hundred missionaries who credit the martyrdom of Jim Elliot, Peter Fleming, Ed McCully, Nate Saint, and Roger Youderian as influencing them to go overseas. Their story is recounted in the movie, *The End of the Spear*, as well as in Elisabeth Elliot's seminal piece, *Through Gates of Splendor*, written a year after the men died.

The men were killed by a fierce tribe in Bolivia whom they were trying to reach with the good news of Jesus Christ. The men left behind five wives and eight children. While in school, Jim Elliot wrote, "O God, save me from a life of barrenness, following a formal pattern of ethics, and give instead that vital contact of soul with Thy divine life that fruit may be produced, and Life-abundant living may be known again as the final proof for Christ's message and work."

He wondered, "'He makes His ministers a flame of fire.' Am I ignitable? God deliver me from the dread asbestos of 'other things.' Saturate me with the oil of the Spirit that I may be aflame. But a flame is transient, often short-lived. Canst thou bear this, my soulshort life? In me there dwells the Spirit of the Great Short-Lived, whose zeal for God's house consumed Him."[236]

After the murders, several men from the Waodanis tribe who were responsible for the men's deaths reported hearing "strange supernatural voices and seeing moving lights in the sky during the attack, as if God sent an angelic choir to celebrate the faithfulness and the homecoming of His loyal servants."[237]

Incredibly, in 1958, two women who were family of the murdered men moved back to the same territory, eventually gaining the trust of the tribe, who came to understand that just as the foreign men were killed, Jesus had been slain for their sins. Many in the tribe soon came to embrace Christ as the Messiah. How different life is when we leave behind the performance based mentality of legalism and rule driven religion.

Ignatius, who was a close friend of the Apostle John, was tortured and martyred in AD 107. He shared, "I would rather die for Christ than rule the whole earth. Leave me to the beasts that I may by them be a partaker of God. Welcome nails and cross, welcome broken bones, welcome all diabolical torture, if I may but obtain the Lord Jesus Christ."[238]

Have you been worn out and exhausted by constantly trying to be "good enough?" Then rest in Jesus, in the promise that even in our sin, he is drawing us to himself, pouring his mercy into our hearts. His call is not complicated; he promises that if we seek, we find; if we knock, the door is opened; and if we ask, we receive.[239] He promises to find us when we have given up on everything else and just surrendered to his amazing grace.

During Marine Corps boot camp, I witnessed a fascinating experiment. The drill instructors said that 10% of people never listen or learn from their mistakes. To make their point, they had us stand in formation in front of our lockers. They explained they would give a simple instruction; our job was to follow their command, and to do nothing more and nothing less.

"You have 30 seconds to grab a pair of socks and running shoes out of your locker. Go!" Eighty recruits then rushed to open their combination locks and return to the painted line on the ground before the drill instructor finished counting down, "three...two...one!"

Once back in formation, we were told to look around, and sure enough, while most men had done as they were ordered, there were a few who held in their hands towels, water, and one even had an MRE.[240]

"We are going to do this one more time, only this time, any failure on your part will mean we are going on a five-mile run. You know the rules, so pay attention. This time, go to your locker and grab you backpack and one canteen of water. Go!"

This time, along with the shuffling of feet, there were many voices repeating out loud what the drill instructor said. "Come on everyone, do it right; otherwise, we will be running all night!" There was the familiar countdown, "three...two...one!" followed by the rush to return to formation.

One by one, recruits presented their backpack and canteen of water, but it wasn't long before the drill instructor found men holding two canteens, some had come back in line with their running shoes, and another had completely forgotten to grab his backpack. Defeated, we marched out of the barracks and into the woods, prepared for the long run before us, a consequence of people who fail to pay attention.

David was someone who had spiritual eyes to see things differently than other people, he paid attention to what God was doing, and moved his life in sync with heaven. The prophet records that before facing Goliath, David "took his staff in his hand, *and chose five smooth stones from the stream.*"[241]

We know from the account that Goliath was in the valley, and the two would battle there. Where do the giants show up? When we are at the lowest point; when we find ourselves in the valley. Why did David choose five stones? Because where there is one giant, there are two; and where there are two, there are three. Samuel tells us Goliath had four brothers, and each "fell by the hand of David."[242] Five giants, five stones, one hero with faith in the protection of heaven, and once again, the light overcoming the darkness.

The giants represented evil and the power of the enemy. David represented the overcomer who can do all things through Christ who gives us strength. It is the difference between seeing ourselves as small before Goliath, or in seeing how small the giants are in compared to God. The lessons of life continue to point to this promise, but we often fail to learn from the instructors that life places before us.

In photography, there are three key rules to taking a better picture that also apply to daily choices. First, you have to be clear on the subject you want to capture. This will determine the type of equipment you will need. For example, to capture wildlife, you will need a telephoto lens, while a scenic shot will require a wide angle lens. When you know your subject, you will be clear on how to implement the next two steps.

In life, we each must decide what target we are trying to hit. What is our mission for our marriage, in our career, as a parent, and in our health and finances? We need to be sure to have a clear and descriptive picture of the outcome we desire.

The second step is to focus on your subject. Every person who views your image should be able to immediately know the purpose of your photograph. When someone looks at your picture in confusion and you have to say, "See, there in the corner, there is a small deer," you have failed to bring focus to your subject. How do you make the subject stand out? You make it the biggest part of the image, you center it, you place extra light on it, you bathe it in bright colors, and you ensure the eyes are in perfect focus, because if the eyes are out of focus the image is lost.

The same things applies to choices; we have to get laser-like focus to make the changes that need to be made, using all the resources available to us, and seeking help when we don't have all the tools we require.

Two important keys to focus are *consistency* and *momentum*. Without consistency, we are simply waiting on the mood to catch up to us to continue towards a goal. If you work towards a healthy marriage or a fit body haphazardly, you will see little growth. But consistency will bring a breakthrough to even the most difficult situation.

After interviewing hundreds of people who transformed their physiques, trainer Anthony Ellis said there was one common denominator these men and women possessed, and that was *consistency*. Compared to the average person trying to lose weight who often overestimates the amount of exercise they do and underestimates the amount of food they consume, those who reach their goals practice consistency. Ellis writes, "Day in and day out, they were consistent with their diet and training schedule. That is the secret to success – in anything!"[243]

Likewise, after losing 65 pounds and becoming a fitness inspiration and instructor, Kaelin Tuell Poulin noted, "If you're going to resist temptation and stay on course, you'll need to embrace the law of results. Results don't just happen; you must consistently do the actions required to achieve the results you want. That's how the law works: if you do the work, you'll see the results."[244]

When a stonecutter finds a boulder, he will begin to hit it with an anvil over and over again. Each day, he may hit the rock twenty times, day in and day out. On the outside, there is no discernable change to the boulder, but the stonecutter knows that if he continues to apply the right pressure, sooner or later, the stone will crack open. When it does break, be it on the one thousandth hit or the five hundredth, it breaks open all at once, crumbling into pieces. That is the power of consistency.

Jack Canfield says to *practice the rule of five*. He quotes Ron Scolastico who told him, "If you would go every day to a very large tree and take five swings at it with a very sharp ax eventually, no matter how large the tree, it would have to come down."[245] No matter how big the obstacle you face is, if you keep moving forward you will find victory, you just have to trust the process. Leonardo da Vinci once drew one thousand hands in a single sitting in an attempt to master drawing the human figure.[246] That is the difference of practicing excellence: taking the life we have been given and consistently seeking to make it a work of art.

Momentum is also absolutely critical. It is much easier to keep moving than it is to keep starting over and over again. When a rocket is trying to break gravity, it consumes 50 to 75 percent of its fuel on takeoff; once it is off the ground, it needs much less energy to continue its forward motion. The same is true in life: once you begin to implement a plan, keep at it until you reach your destination; trying to start over is self-defeating.

I have listened as students in graduate programs report, "I am just going to take one semester off to catch my breath," then never return to complete their degree. Countless people miss a day at the gym, which becomes two days, which soon becomes weeks, and then before long, they have given up all together. This is why momentum is so important; it keeps us on track.

I was recently in a nature photography contest and a man had entered a blurry picture of a black bear climbing a tree under an eagle's nest. When his picture didn't place, he angrily scolded the judges. "This is a rare image; how many times has someone taken a picture of a black bear under a nest like that?"

"I don't know," the judge answered, trying to determine if the black blob was indeed a bear. "The problem, sir, is the image is so out of focus, it is virtually worthless as a photograph."

Irritated, the man snapped back, "This is a rare image; you don't know what you are talking about! This photo was very hard to get, I hiked in the woods for hours before I spotted this bear, and then I had to wait patiently for the perfect opportunity to take the picture as he started climbing!"

The judge calmly replied, "What you have here is a potentially interesting story, and if this were a story contest, you might have placed. However, this is a photography contest, and you will never place with a poor quality image, no matter what details you provide about how you got the shot."

The man snatched his photo from the judge's hand and stormed off. But the judge was absolutely correct. If you want a quality picture, it has to be in razor-sharp focus. You want a different quality of life? Then in the same vein, you must be focused on your outcome and abide by the spiritual laws that are in place, including using the tools of consistency and momentum. Otherwise, you are trying to bend the universe to your own way of thinking and you will never make progress towards what you really want.

The third step to a better picture is to eliminate the clutter. If you take an image of something and the background is distracting, you need to take the shot from a different angle to remove the distractions or crop out the background material on the computer. Another technique is to produce a shallow depth of field by using the correct lens, which will blur the background while keeping your subject in focus.

The principle is obvious: what pulls us away from our destiny needs to find an exit from our life. That may include removing, or at least limiting, the access of toxic people. As Levine notes, "We give our time away all day long, to emotions that gain us no advantage, to people who do not value our time."[247] It may mean simplifying our lifestyle so we can be more financially free, which brings more choices for how we spend our time.

In the gospels, Jesus condemns the city of Bethsaida because they refused to repent.[248] Later, there is an account of a blind man from that same city searching for healing. The people with the man also begged Jesus to give the man sight. Mark records that before healing this person, "Jesus took the blind man by the hand and led him outside the village."[249] He did this to remove the man from the presence of people filled with doubt and negativity.

When Dodie Osteen was told by her doctor that she had cancer, she began to write out as many scriptures on healing as she could find. She found a photograph of herself at her healthiest and posted it by her bed. Then she regularly in prayer confessed and envisioned herself as healed. Of the experience, she wrote, "When you are believing for a miracle, it is imperative you surround yourself only with those who support you."[250] We need to steer clear of people who contaminate the environment of faith and cause clutter in our lives.

There is a process to growth, and part of that process is trusting that if you work the plan, the plan will work. Spiritually, it is about trusting that there is a hand that guides us, at times even into the furnace of affliction, so that our spiritual muscles are forced to grow as we face giants and bigger challenges. David's goal was clear: remove the giants. He wisely chose his weapons of war and focused on the task at hand. Lastly, he removed the clutter, *his brothers' voices of fear and criticism*, from his ears.

Too many quit at the first sign of discomfort. So, instead of hitting the mission field they dreamed about, they stay home. Instead of pursuing a degree, they convince themselves there is no use. Instead of practicing forgiveness, they tell themselves it won't make a difference anyway, so why try. We can make excuses for almost anything.

Over the years, my wife and I have had the privilege of working hand in hand with some of the most elite instructors in the dog and horse training world. Of the latter, we have especially enjoyed the work of Clinton Anderson. When it comes to horses, he states that "the worst, most dangerous, most disrespectful horse in the world wasn't born that way...he was born into this world with no opinions, no habits, and no perceptions. What happened in his world since that moment determined how he behaved."[251]

What works with horses and dogs that carry a lot of baggage? Calm, compassionate leadership that allows the animal to know it doesn't need to be anxious or afraid. A presence of strength relaxes the animal, and they no longer feel the need to be on the lookout for danger. Then they connect with people much more easily and are able to receive instruction.

Often, we carry a story around about the past, about why things are the way they are, or why they can't change. We have to overcome those limitations, and allow healing to take place where it needs to happen so we are no longer inhibited by moments and circumstances from prior months and years.

Along this line of thinking, there is a fascinating experiment that shows how unfounded fears hold people back. Researches placed four monkeys in a room that was centered on a pole. At the top of the pole was a bunch of bananas. Each time a monkey began to climb the pole to retrieve a banana, the researchers sprayed him with cold water, causing him to abandon his pursuit of the forbidden fruit. Eventually, the monkeys stopped trying to climb the pole.

Then something amazing happened when a new monkey was introduced to the group. As suspected, the newcomer went right towards the pole and began to head towards the bananas. Before he could make the climb, the other monkeys grabbed him and pulled him back down! One by one, the researches replaced the original monkeys with new monkeys, with each newcomer being prohibited from climbing the pole by the other fearful monkeys.

A remarkable discovery was made by this experiment. In the end, *all* the original monkeys were out of the room and only new monkeys were left, monkeys who never got sprayed by the cold water or ever saw the hose. Still, they refused to try to climb the pole, having no idea why![252]

How many people refuse to try with no idea why they feel so paralyzed other than someone else told them it wasn't worth it? How many dreams have been abandoned because well-meaning people made harsh comments or talked someone else back down to ground level where it was "safe?" As Morehouse notes, "Most of us spend the vast majority of our lives looking backward into the past dwelling on the illusion of some event that we choose to keep giving energy. We assign emotion and belief to the past and accept some identity based on that emotion."[253]

This is why we need to continually evaluate our thinking and our perceptions. Richard Bandler notes, "If you learn as a child to be afraid of strangers – that might be useful or it might not be. As an adult, you have to go out and meet people. Fear of strangers becomes paranoia in the extreme. That might be a behavior you want to dispose of. You might want to substitute, 'I am curious about people' as a new self-representation."[254] This is why intentional growth and evaluation are so important, we uncover beliefs and rules that no longer meet our needs.

How much different the road to authentic progress is when we walk into the unknown trusting in a higher identity; controlling our fear, not always knowing the outcome but fully believing that we will never be the same. The past need not control today.

In the thirteenth century, Francis of Assisi expressed his desire to grow and live when he declared, "Lord, make me an instrument of your peace. Where there is hatred, let me sow love; where there is injury, pardon; where there is doubt, faith; where there is despair, hope; where there is darkness, light; where there is sadness, joy. O Divine Master, grant that I may not so much seek to be consoled as to console; to be understood as to understand; to be loved as to love. For it is in giving that we receive; it is in pardoning that we are pardoned; it is in dying that we are born to eternal life."

One day, the Pharisees attempted to trap Jesus in a public debate, asking if it was right to pay taxes to Rome who had long oppressed the Israelites. Some estimates say that in Judah, a family paid 50% of their income in taxes to the Roman Empire. The money went to funding the military's exuberant building projects and the lavish lifestyles of the government officials. Clearly, it was a sensitive area of discussion in Jerusalem, and the Pharisees believed they could turn some people against Jesus for his answer.

The Pharisees taught they were a set apart group, even dressing specifically to clearly distinguish themselves from everyone else. Though some had a fervent faith, many who encountered Jesus simply practiced a religion that brought little change to their hearts. At one point, Jesus warned the crowds, "When you give to the needy, do not announce it with trumpets, as the hypocrites do in the synagogues,"[255] a reference to the practice of some Pharisees.

The Temple contained 13 containers to collect alms for the poor. Each container was shaped like a trumpet and made a noticeable sound when coins were dropped into them. Some of the religious leaders would place several coins in at the same time, making a lot of noise and gaining a lot of attention. The practice was known as *sounding the trumpet*.[256] It was one more occasion where Jesus pointed out the difference between religious practice and authentic faith. These impromptu lessons for the crowds offended the Pharisees who often found themselves painted unfavorably in Jesus' messages.[257]

In confronting him, they were hoping a discussion about taxes would win some converts from his followers, as there was tremendous disapproval of the government. In response Jesus asked for a coin. One side the coin bore an image of the head of Tiberius Caesar along with the inscription, "Tiberius Caesar, son of the divine Augustus." The flip side showed a picture of Pax, the Roman goddess of peace, along with the words "High Priest" in Latin.

Holding the coin Jesus asked whose image was inscribed upon it. Everyone knew it was the Caesar's. (By the 1st Century Julius Caesar's name had become a title for all Roman Emperors, and at the time of Jesus' ministry Tiberius was in charge.) Once the crowd and the Pharisees acknowledged Tiberius' image was stamped upon the coin Jesus replied, "Give to Caesar what is Caesar's, and to God what is God's."[258] The crowd was left speechless.

The question each of us must ask is, "Whose image do I bear? Which king is ruling my life right now?" All people were created in God's image and all are called to give their life to him. Many have exchanged that image for something else, be it greed or pleasure or self or any other thing. In Christ, we have all been offered a way out of the prison of sin and self.

In the late nineteenth century, John Hyde moved to India to share the gospel. Having suffered the loss of his brother, he felt it best to give his own life to reach the lost with the gift of love. He faced much opposition in his outreach, and in turn gave his life to prayer as his only hope. So heavy was his heart for reaching lost people, he often gave up food and sleep to intercede with heaven on their behalf. When he died at 47 of untreatable cancer, his last words were in Punjabi, "Bol, Yisu' Masih, Ki Jai." Translated to English, his final message was, "Shout, the victory of Jesus Christ!"[259]

Scripture uses various ways to describe this new life. In the gospel of John it is known as a new birth, of passing from darkness to light. In Luke, it is going from being dead to being alive, from being lost to being found. In Paul's letters it is known as becoming a new creation. Each of these metaphors point to Jesus' invitation to live a life in a different dimension, moving from the mundane to the miraculous. There we find faith, hope, and love, if we but heed the call of his still, small voice inside. There we can daily declare over our self as Mark Hendrickson writes, "Jesus became the curse so that I don't have the bear the curse."[260]

There is a little-known but fascinating piece of history that involves the Mount of Olives where Jesus was crucified and where he was resurrected. The Midrash reports that on the Mount of Olives, the Shekinah glory of God appeared and remained there for three and a half *years* leading up to the destruction of the Temple in AD 70. A voice was said to be heard from the cloud calling the nation to repentance. People believed the voice was *Bet Kol*, the very voice of God.[261]

Another lost witness for many people in the West is found every year at the Eastern Orthodox Church celebration of Easter. In Jerusalem, a priest enters the tomb where Jesus is believed to have been buried. It is known as the celebration of the "uncreated light." There before thousands of witnesses, a light flashes from within the tomb and candles are supernaturally lit. The fire doesn't burn even as the flames grow amongst the crowd.[262] These are simply more examples of the divine life calling people to the living waters.

When writing to his daughter, George McDonald, C.S. Lewis' mentor, penned; "God is so beautiful, and so patient, and so loving, and so generous that he is the heart and soul and rock of every love and every kindness and every gladness in the world. All the beauty in the world and in the hearts of men, all the painting, all the poetry, all the music, all the architecture comes out of his heart first. He is so loveable that no heart can know how loveable he is, can only know in part. When the best loves God best, he does not love him nearly as he deserves, or as he will love him in time."[263]

Even history's darkest moment was filled with the presence and goodness of God. The gospels tell us that Jesus carried his cross "to a place called Golgotha (which means The Place of the Skull)."[264] (The oft-used word "Calvary" is simply Latin for *skull*.) Some believe the name is derived from the shape of the mountain, others have claimed it was given due to the number of executions that have taken place there. However, there is no mountain shaped like a skull in Jerusalem, and in the text Matthew is clearly referencing *one* skull.

Much more telling is an understanding of the origin of the name from ancient history as well as the Eastern Orthodox Church. Tradition holds that Golgotha was known as "The Place of the Skull" because Adam's skull was found there. This is why many paintings of the crucifixion have a skull at the base of the cross. The pictures represent that Jesus was crucified on the very spot where Adam was buried.

Paul wrote, "The first man Adam became a living being; the last Adam, a life-giving spirit."[265] Jesus, the second life-giving Adam, died where the first Adam died. Where Adam was buried, Jesus was crucified to bring life. As Luther declared, "The cross alone is our theology."[266] *However*, Jesus came to reverse the fall and did not remain in the grave.

Though Adam's skull represented death, Jesus blood on that very same spot represented the birth of eternal life. This is why the crowds cried out "hallelujah" and "hosanna!" when Jesus rode into Jerusalem. They understood that even the long held darkness was being replaced by the light. As Max Lucado writes, "When God became flesh, he fought for your soul. When Jesus faced the devil in the wilderness, he fought for your peace. When he stood up for the neglected, was he not standing up for you? When he died on the cross for your sins, he fought for your salvation. When he left the Holy Spirit to guide, strengthen, and comfort you, he was fighting for your life."[267]

Sometimes, the most important thing to do is simply stop and feel gratitude for such grace. You can also focus on the people in your life and the gifts you have received from heaven's hand. As Homer W. Hodge beautifully stated, "Prayer should be the breath of our breathing, the thought of our thinking, the soul of our feeling, and the life of our living, the sound of our hearing, the growth of our growing."[268]

You might notice your breath as well, slowly breathing in and breathing out, taking in the good and releasing the negative. As you do, whisper one of the oldest prayers known from church history, "Lord Jesus Christ, Son of God, have mercy on me, a sinner," and then smile, knowing that it is done. More recently, Father Mateo offered this simple prayer to use, "Jesus, come deliver your people. Jesus, come heal the sick."[269] Others suggest repeating, "Come Holy Spirit."[270]

It is about having a quiet focus, away from the distractions that so easily consume. Andrew Murray said the *secret* to a life in prayer lay in taking "time in the inner chamber to bow down and worship; and wait on Him until He unveils Himself, and takes possession of you, and goes out with you to show how a man can live and walk in abiding fellowship with an unseen Lord."

Some see the breath "as a transportation system"[271] and purposefully exhale or blow out negative thoughts and feelings with every breath they release, inwardly observing the negative thoughts dissolve with each exhalation. Consciously slowing your breath while inhaling deeply works for several reasons. Our body instinctively responds to stress with the fight, flight, or freeze response. When these stress reactions happen, we get physically tense, our heart rate increases, and our breathing becomes shallow to preserve precious oxygen. The freeze instinct also slows our breathing as the body seeks to keep as still as possible so as to go unnoticed by an approaching predator.

In contrast, we only take deep, slow breaths when we feel safe. So, when we take control of our breathing, slowing it down on purpose, noticing each inhalation and exhalation, we are telling ourselves there is nothing to fear. Add gratitude to this quietness, and you will experience a new sense of peace.

Spurgeon wrote, "Prayer and praise are like the breathing in and out of air and make up that spiritual respiration by which the inner life is instrumentally supported. We take in an inspiration of heavenly air as we pray; we breathe it out again in praise unto God from whom it came."

When scripture talks about meditating, the word contains the idea of chewing; to absorb slowly what is on the page as one who is deliberately tasting each morsel of food. The term also implies to reflect mentally as you rehear the words in your thoughts, as well as to verbally rehearse a verse by speaking it forth.[272]

Grant Jeffrey writes; "When an ambassador of an African prince was introduced to Queen Victoria, he asked her the question his monarch had requested he present to her: "What is the secret of your country's power and success throughout the world?" Queen Victoria picked up a Bible and answered, 'Tell your prince that this book is the secret of England's greatness.'"[273] Such is the power of scripture, "Sharper than any double-edged sword, it penetrates even to dividing soul and spirit, joints and marrow; it judges the thoughts and attitudes of the heart."[274]

One place to begin using the Bible is to take a chapter from the Book of Psalms and purposefully consider each word while quietly reading through the verses. Many also find it useful to read one chapter of Proverbs a day throughout the month; chapter 1 on day one, chapter 2 on day two, and so on. Lastly, when you study history, you will find that the Book of Romans is a key text that has helped people more fully understand the grace of God. Spending the next 6 months daily chewing on these three books will do wonders for your spiritual life.

As Jackie Buckingham said, "Your heart believes. Your heart has faith. Your heart hears God is a God of miracles, and He is going to heal you. But your head—your mind—is listening to Satan. Satan doesn't speak to your heart—that's where God reigns supreme. He speaks to your mind...That's the reason it is so important that we fill our mind with God, with the Word of God, that we keep our minds fixed on Him."[275]

There is strength in mixing inspired scripture with the power of breath and gratitude. It is trusting that moment to moment the life-giving Adam is always with you. As Tennyson wrote, "Closer is He than breathing, and nearer than hands and feet."

CHAPTER 7

WHEN FAITH BECOMES SIGHT

"It is a serious thing to live in a society of possible gods and goddesses, to remember that the dullest most uninteresting person you talk to may one day be a creature which, if you saw it now, you would be strongly tempted to worship."

– **C. S. Lewis**

At well over 6 feet tall, with hands the size of a catcher's mitt, Doug was truly a giant of a man. His family had an Amish background, and he still held on to some of their ideals of simple living. While he had his own farm, he was not completely averse to modern technology. It was December 31st, and my wife casually asked if he had plans for New Year's Day.

With tears in his eyes, he quietly explained that he always stayed home for this particular holiday. It had been ten years since his wife walked out the door without warning. The only time he had heard from her since then was a short phone conversation four years ago when she called him on January 1st. "Who knows, maybe she will call again, so I will be home sitting next to my phone, just in case."

In 1952, Florence Chadwick wanted to swim California's shoreline. She had already been the first woman to swim the English Channel. On the day of the swim, her fear eventually got the best of her. Scared of sharks, fighting the fog and the chilly water, she told the boat beside her she wanted to quit. She had already been swimming for fifteen hours, and exhausted she was ready to throw in the towel. Her mother tried to encourage her, telling her she was close, but panicked Chadwick gave up.[276]

She later told a reporter, "All I could see was the fog...I think if I could have seen the shore, I would have made it." In reality, she was very close to the shore when she quit. Fortunately, she was successful at her next attempt and has inspired generations ever since.[277]

The difficulty in the haze is the uncertainty of the outcome when we can't see the other side. It may be hoping for the return of a spouse who left in the middle of the night. It could be waiting on a doctor to share the results of a test, or it may simply be a time where a person feels like they just can't take another step, either way the fog is very real.

In the late 1800s, Horatio Spafford was a prominent lawyer in Chicago. He and his family lost nearly everything in the city's great fire. Several months later, he planned a trip to England. Traveling by boat, his wife and four daughters went ahead of him while Horatio stayed behind to finish some last-minute business. Tragically, their ship was struck by an ocean liner, and all four children were killed. Horatio received a telegram from his wife with two words, "Saved alone."

Immediately, Horatio boarded a ship to head to England to be with his wife. The captain of his boat stopped the ship at the location of the accident and called Horatio on deck. As Horatio studied the ocean spot where he lost it all, he quietly went below deck and penned the following words:

> *When peace, like a river, attendeth my way*
> *When sorrows like sea billows roll*
> *Whatever my lot, thou hast taught me to say*
> *It is well, it is well with my soul.*

At times the road before us is so unclear. That is why the writers of the New Testament often stressed the power of *today* and of learning to live with moment-to-moment gratitude. Paul would use athletic terms to describe the spiritual journey. He spoke of running a race, of boxing and training and sweat. In the book of Ephesians, Paul wrote, "We are God's *workmanship*, created in Christ Jesus to do good works, which God prepared in advance for us to do."[278] The word that the apostle uses for "workmanship" is the word from which we get *poem* in English. We are God's poem, his masterpiece, a work of art. Every life is called to express the image of God.

For Paul, following Jesus meant laying everything on the line, just as an Olympian training for the games pushes his body to the limit. His view of being a disciple was far from the boring picture many people paint with their lives. His own life was a witness to this commitment.

To Corinth he would share, "From the Jews five times I received forty stripes minus one. Three times I was beaten with rods; once I was stoned; three times I was shipwrecked; a night and a day I have been in the deep."[279]

The whip he describes here would have contained three cords, often made of donkey or cow hide. Beatings would include contact with the face, back and the legs. If he was indeed beaten with three cords, he would have received 117 lashings at each beating. This would mean he had a total of 585 scars on his body.[280] It is perhaps for this reason he would also write, "Finally, let no one cause me trouble, for I bear on my body the marks of Jesus."[281]

Handel loved to play music, but he found audiences hard to please, taking their criticisms especially hard. Sometimes England's crowds didn't even show up to hear him play. In 1741, heartbroken and ill, he decided to retire. Mineral baths did little to alleviate the sickness that left him partially paralyzed, leaving him with little hope.

Later that same year, a friend named Charles Jennings gave him a booklet on the life of Christ to set to music. Unimpressed, Handel read through the text. His eyes eventually fell on the words, "I know that my redeemer lives."[282] He would go on to share that at that moment the presence of God was almost palpable, and hope returned to his body and spirit. Since the Redeemer lives, he can meet all our deepest needs.

For the next three weeks, Handel wrote non-stop, completing what has been called the greatest feet in the history of music composition. We know his masterpiece as *Messiah*.[283] When it was first played, the king rose from his chair and applauded, and today, we still stand when we hear the song.

Paul would have been familiar with the same words as the composer, "I know that my redeemer lives." He would live and die to tell people the secret to life was found in the indwelling Christ.

When he was beaten with rods three times, it was an attempt by the authorities to leave him unable to walk—a punishment normally reserved for those who broke the law. The criminal would be tied up, then lifted into the air by their legs, at which point they would be beaten upon the soles of their feet until they turned bloody. Paul's crime was telling people about Jesus. How much more meaningful his words are to the church in Rome, "How beautiful are the feet of those who bring good news!"[284]

People often give up and walk away at the slightest bit of discomfort. The gospel calls us to a higher standard, a standard that refuses to back down in the face of opposition, refusing to be intimidated. It is in such times we need to remember that Christ is always with us, and that in him, we have nothing to fear.

Not long ago, we had a new neighbor move in next door during the winter months. It was several weeks before I had a chance to knock on the door and introduce myself. The occupants were a young couple with a small infant. We exchanged pleasantries and committed to getting to know each other better when the weather warmed up.

About a week later, I was at my local gym and a man greeted me. Realizing I didn't recognize him he said, "Remember me, I am your new neighbor?" Embarrassed, I knew there was no recovering from such a mistake, at least not that day. Feeling like a heel, I went home and told my wife what had happened. I resolved to find him again at the gym and try to make up for my carelessness.

Sure enough, I saw him about two weeks later and said hello, shared a few polite comments, and went on my way. But I told my wife I was not satisfied yet, that I didn't think my feeble effort had cancelled out my glaring omission weeks earlier when I failed to recognize this man. To make a long story short, it would be about three weeks before I would catch him at the gym again, making a point to say hello, chatting briefly, and moving on to my work out. Three more times that winter, we exchanged a few words when running into each other before exercising.

Before long spring was setting in and the weather was warming up. I was outside one day when my new neighbor walked out with his dog. Again we talked for a few minutes, exchanging the normal grunts and small talk that men pass off as "conversation." As he gathered up his dog and departed, I watched as he walked back into his house, then turned to my wife and said, "Honey, that is *not* the guy I have been talking to at the gym!"

J.M. Barrie said, "We are all failures—at least, all the best of us are." Each of us has times when we wish we could have done things differently, where we felt foolish or knew the sting of regret; but the real question is whether or not we give up when the rods and stones knock us down.

When the apostle wrote that he spent a night and a day in the *deep*, his words indicate the deepest part of the ocean. The memories he was calling to mind were surely still fresh. For a while I lived in Okinawa. For the most part the water was very clear, and we would often swim out to the coral to explore the magnificent creatures found there. However, between the shore and the reef, there was a particular section thirty yards long where the water was so murky you could not see what was below. At times, the trip through this area was incredibly frightening.

Many men and women know what it is like to find themselves out in the deep, treading water all night, alone in the dark. It seems like no one else understands, or that they are so consumed with their own problems, they hardly notice our struggle to stay above the surface. On nights like these, a God far away brings little comfort. Thus, Jesus broke into our world and promised to live in us, so we face nothing alone because "whoever is united with the Lord is one with him in spirit."[285] Norman Grubb described how this works out in reality when he shared, "A crisis comes to me. No, no—it doesn't! It comes to *us*. Not to me, but to *us*...It comes to Him...He's going to turn it out for His own purposes. So what is my attitude? 'Come on Lord, handle it now. Praise the Lord, it's perfect! Carry it out now—I'll watch you.'"[286]

Perhaps for you it is a friend's betrayal, a divorce, or a lost dream. The gospel message is that Christ is right there in the midst of your aloneness, he is there in the deep with you. Emerson once said, "People are always getting ready to live but never living." Many are drifting in the ocean, wondering if anyone even notices. Yet when you find yourself in the deepest, darkest sea, know there is a nail pierced hand holding on to you. As John Newton noted, "Much depends on the way we come into trouble. Paul and Jonah were both in a storm, but in very different circumstances." True faith is about trusting the ever abiding presence of Christ, even when facing the biggest waves.

In 1942, John Wilfinger served as a missionary in Borneo, south of Australia. At the time Japanese forces were taking foreign hostages on the island, and John learned he and his fellow workmen were a priority on their list.

Rather than risk villagers' lives, John and his friends decided to turn themselves in to the Japanese authorities. Hoping to find his fiancée first, John stopped at a few villages along the way before finally surrendering. Three days later, he was executed just hours after Christmas for the crime of spreading the gospel. At the end of the war, his body and his Bible were recovered. A poem was found inside that read:

> No mere man is the Christ I know
> But greater far than all below.
> Day by day his love enfolds me
> Day by day his power upholds me.
> All that God could ever be
> The man of Nazareth is to me.

No mere man can my strength sustain
And drive away all fear and pain.
Holding me close in his embrace
When death and I stand face to face.
Then all that God could ever be
The unseen Christ will be for me.

Underneath the poem, he wrote, "Hallelujah, this is real."[287]

We tried houses and cars. When that didn't work, we got better houses and cars. Incidentally, research is clear about the relationship between money and happiness. We often think that *just a little bit more* will be enough. However, that little bit more makes little to no difference after a person reaches an income of $100,000.[288] Anything beyond that amount just doesn't increase our feeling of wellbeing, in spite of how the media celebrates the supposed lifestyles of a few millionaires.

I worked at a company where they gave out "manager's chairs" that were a little bit larger than the chairs the rest of the staff used. Another company handed out five-dollar bills to the employees who showed the most spirit at the weekly meeting. Such shallow attempts at motivation and self-importance leave little wonder that in the climate we have created people struggle to find the lasting answers they are looking for.

Some people have children for selfish reasons, believing they can somehow create the unconditional love they crave. When one doesn't seem to bring the answer, they try having a second child. However, contrary to popular opinion, studies show that having children can actually *lower* a couple's happiness level in the majority of cases.[289] This is not to discount that for some, it is the most fulfilling purpose in their life, but it is to suggest we stop just repeating the actions of other people without taking into consideration whether these popular ideas and philosophies hold water.

Some women become so enmeshed in the lives of their children, they have no identity left of their own. For men, it is common to immerse themselves in work and promotions, believing perhaps a new title or a bigger office will bring deeper satisfaction. Once we obtain what we think we want, the paradox is that the feeling of being unsatisfied still exists, so we try something else only to be disappointed again. It is a seemingly endless cycle. This is why Twyman notes, "Time after time this process is repeated until you finally come to a profound realization: There's nothing in the *outside* world that can satisfy the longing you feel."[290]

It has been said that Christ is all that remains when we have tried everything else and have come to the end of our self. When all our support systems have failed, we are at a place where we can gratefully realize the truth, "When God is all you have left, you have everything you need."

There is an ancient story about a rich man in Baghdad who sends his servant to the market. Shortly thereafter the servant returns in great fear. His master asks him what has frightened him, and the servant explains that while at the market, Death was there and gave him a look. Terrified, the servant asks for a horse to flee town to stay in Samaria. The master agrees, but before long, his curiosity overtakes him and he soon finds himself at the market looking for Death. It doesn't take him long to spot the sinister presence. He approaches and asks why Death chose to frighten his servant. Death replies, "I didn't mean to startle him. It was me who was surprised to see him here, for tonight, I have an appointment with him in Samaria."

Today is the day to stop being pleased with far too little. Today is the day to raise your standards, to commit more, to love more, and pray for a deeper faith and revelation of what it means to be united with Christ.

For better or for worse, the following words have either liberated or haunted humanity since the beginning of time: "A man reaps what he sows."[291] It is a universal law that leaves the responsibility of a person's life in their own hands. As Bo Lozoff states, "Every thought, word, and deed is a seed which we plant in the world. All our lives, we harvest the fruit of those seeds. If we plant desire, greed, fear, anger and doubt, then that's what will fill our lives. Plant love, courage, understanding, good humor, and that's what we get back. This isn't negotiable, it's a law of energy, just like gravity."[292] Lozoff continues that when we fail to learn the lessons of the harvests we have created, we are literally listing a "Teaching Wanted" ad in the spiritual classifieds, inviting another experience into our life to impart often painful lessons until we wake up.[293]

On the one hand, this truth brings great freedom. What do you want more of in your life? Begin to give that which you want to receive. Need more love? Give more love. Need more kindness? Begin to act in such a way. Need a financial breakthrough? You will need to begin giving money to other people who are in need, trusting that in return, you will receive what you give, even if you don't know how it will work out.

One teacher I know practices this principle when it comes to prayer. When someone asks him to pray for their need, he has them pray for someone else first. It is about being intentional in our choices and intentional about our growth. It means paying attention to the results our current decisions are producing, and making wise choices that will move us closer to the life we desire and deserve.

It is important to note that we don't necessarily reap *when* we sow. It is safe to say that our lives today are the result of choices and actions we made six months ago. Where do you want to be six months from now? Begin sowing the right actions today, so that when those seeds become a harvest, you will reap the benefits. As Avanzini notes, "Do not sow your seed one day and expect to reap a harvest the next morning. Would a farmer plant his crops on Thursday, and then on Friday take his combine out into the field expecting a harvest?"[294]

We also have no guarantee we will reap *where* we so. We may give love to someone and they give little in return. Our job is to know that we will eventually receive back what we gave, and that God will work out the source of that blessing.

Desi Williamson grew up in a very rough neighborhood with a mother addicted to drugs. His brothers were constantly in trouble with the law, one spending years in jail and the other being paralyzed from the neck down after being shot.

One day, his brother was in his wheelchair deep in thought. Desi asked what he was thinking about, and his brother told him about the dreams he used to have and all the things he planned to change. He cried as he said that he was paying a terrible price for not making better choices. Desi's brother then looked him in the eye and said, "Desi, it's not enough to just change! Man, you've got to change in time!"[295] Don't wait to begin sowing towards the life you want to live. *Different standards, different life.*

In biblical times, when a young man fell in love with a young woman, he would propose to her in public in front of their families by placing a glass of wine on a banquet table. If she said yes to the engagement, she would take the glass in hand, then the groom would immediately head to his father's house and begin to build an addition for himself and his new bride. This process took about a year. After he completed the new dwelling, his father would inspect it to be sure it was suitable.

With his father's approval, he would then head to his bride's home with the sounding of a shofar, where he would find her waiting with her oil lamp burning bright. Together, they would lead a joyful procession back to their new home for the marriage ceremony and celebration to take place.

When Jesus and his followers gathered on the final night before he was crucified, his disciples were frightened and grieved by what was about to happen. Jesus said to them, "Do not let your hearts be troubled. Trust in God; trust also in me. In my Father's house are many rooms; if it were not so, I would have told you. I am going there to prepare a place for you. And if I go and prepare a place for you, I will come back and take you to be with me that you also may be where I am."[296]

As Jesus painted a picture of what the next several hours would hold, he used the familiar metaphor of a wedding, an occasion of joy. Just like the relationship of a bride and groom, he would go and build his followers rooms in his Father's mansion, then one day come and take them to be with him in a grand celebration. It was an image they could relate to, a picture of hope and anticipation.[297]

I once counselled a congregation going through its *third* split. They asked me what could be done to "fix" things. I told them they were asking the wrong questions. Things had reached a point where they no longer needed to ask how to repair the damage. It was time to begin asking, *should we even exist as a congregation*.

It was a difficult discussion, one they ultimately ignored, and their problems continued to get worse.

Along with the sad fact that every year 20,000 pastors leave the ministry due to examples like these, studies have shown that *over fifty percent* of pastors' wives were listed as "severely depressed."[298] The way people treat one another is key to the problem. Too often we simply want everyone to agree with us, or to pay a price if they don't. We need to pay much closer attention to the seeds we are sowing, especially in light of the returning groom.

Henri Nouwen talked about the competition to be right with little thought for others. He wrote, "I know the pain of this predicament. In it, everything loses its spontaneity. Everything becomes suspect, self-conscious, calculated, and full of second-guessing. There is no longer any trust. Each little move calls for a countermove; each little remark begs for analysis; the smallest gesture has to be evaluated. This is the pathology of the darkness."[299]

At a recent conference, Ken Blanchard shared about taking an African safari. When they came upon a roaring male lion, the guide explained that the roar could be heard for miles around, telling other animals where his territory begins and ends. Blanchard said the lion was like so many people, yelling, "This is *mine...mine... mine.*" This is the way of the darkness. Far better than *mine* is learning what one speaker calls two of the most comforting words one human can share with another: "me too." As Michael Card notes, "The degree to which I am willing to enter into the suffering of another person reveals the level of my commitment and love for them. If I am not interested in your hurts, I am not really interested in you."[300]

Consequently, Douglas C. Smith offers a powerful strategy to begin to see things differently in other people, as well as in the person in the mirror. Instead of competing with others, think of a person who you know is psychologically wounded, or causes you emotional upset. Once you see them in your mind's eye, write down five gifts you have received from this person by completing the sentence, "This person gives me..."[301]

Paul wrote to the church in Ephesus, "Do not let any unwholesome talk come out of your mouths, but only what is helpful for building others up according to their needs, that it may benefit those who listen."[302] Neil Anderson says that if we memorize and live by these words, half our problems will disappear overnight.[303] Life in the light is very different. There we declare that everything belongs to Jesus. To this end, Paul writes, "I have been crucified with Christ and I no longer live, but Christ lives in me."[304]

Again, right thoughts and right beliefs lead to right actions, and all three are *crucial*. When we more fully understand that we no longer live but Christ lives in us, we can stop the exhausting race to please others, to feel like we are enough, knowing there is often a viscous price to pay when trying to earn other people's approval. Instead we can just rest in knowing that because *he* is, then *we* are.

The Gospel of Matthew records a significant moment during the Last Supper, "And when they had *sung a hymn*, they went out to the Mount of Olives."[305] During Passover, it was common to end the meal by singing Psalm 118.

Jesus had just finished telling his disciples about his impending arrest and crucifixion. In a few hours, crowds would turn violent against him and he would be beaten, mocked, and hung from a tree.

Before they filed out of the upper room, they began to sing the words David wrote in the psalm, "Give thanks to the Lord, for he is good; his love endures forever."[306] The words hung in the air, a peace settling over the men. They continued, "The Lord is with me; I will not be afraid. What can mere mortals do to me?"[307] With eyes closed, faces towards heaven, perhaps there was a special emphasis as they sang the next verse, "I will not die but live, and will proclaim what the Lord has done."[308]

It is a poignant moment in history. Soon the singing would stop, the sound of soldiers marching in a legion would be heard, a kiss of betrayal would be given, and a hostile trial would begin. But for one last moment, before stepping out into the evening air where for a short time "darkness reigns,"[309] they paused and one last time sung, "Give thanks to the Lord, for he is good; his love endures forever."[310]

> Years ago, an unknown writer penned *One Solitary Life*, which reads,
>
> Here is a man who was born in an obscure village as the child of a peasant woman. He grew up in another obscure village. He worked in a carpenter shop until he was thirty and then for three years was an itinerant preacher.
>
> He never wrote a book. He never held an office. He never owned a home. He never had a family. He never went to college. He never put his foot inside a big city. He never traveled two hundred miles from the place where he was born. He never did one of the things that usually accompany greatness. He had no credentials but himself.
>
> While still a young man the tide of popular opinion turned against him. His friends ran away. One of them denied him. Another betrayed him. He was turned over to his enemies. He went through the mockery of a trial. He was nailed upon the

cross between two thieves. His executioners gambled for the only piece of property he had on earth while he was dying, and that was his coat. When he was dead, he was taken down and laid in a borrowed grave through the pity of a friend.

Nineteen wide centuries have come and gone and today he is the center of the human race and the leader of the column of progress. I am far within the mark when I say that all the armies that ever marched, and all the navies that were ever built, and all the parliaments that ever sat and all the kings that ever reigned, put together, have not affected the life of man upon the earth as powerfully as has this one solitary life.[311]

When asked how to start a whole new life and how to radically change society, Rodney "Gypsy" Smith offered, "Go home, lock yourself in your room, kneel down in the middle of your floor. Draw a chalk mark all around yourself and ask God to start the revival inside that chalk mark. When He has answered your prayer, the revival will be on."

At times, the road before us is uncertain, the view is cloudy, and supporters are few. It is then we can begin to sow more intentionally towards the high calling set before us. Because he is always with us, we can proclaim, ""Give thanks to the Lord, for he is good; his love endures forever." Then we begin to see the lessons we are meant to learn so much more clearly.

As Ole Anthony writes,

We pray for patience: God sends tribulation

We pray for submission: God sends suffering

We pray for unselfishness: God asks that we sacrifice

We pray for victory: God allows us to be tempted

We pray for humility: God allows messengers of Satan to buffet us

We pray for strength: God reveals our secret fears and innermost weakness

We pray for union with Jesus: God severs all natural ties and we walk alone and   our friends misunderstand

We pray for love: God sends us peculiar suffering by sending us unlovely people

We pray for likeness to Jesus: God puts us in the furnace of affliction

Much that perplexes us is but an answer to our prayers![312]

CHAPTER 8

A REMARKABLE NEW IDENTITY

"I believe that all government is evil, and that trying to improve it is largely a waste of time."

– H. L. Mencken

A few years ago, a 12-year-old girl was kidnapped in Ethiopia. Her captors were seven men who hadn't decided yet whether they were going to force her into marriage or sell her as a slave. For seven days, they marched her through the jungle where she was regularly beaten.

Finally, a week into her abduction, the girl saw a chance to break free of the men and run away. As she did, the men gave chase. Seemingly out of nowhere, a pride of lions rushed out of the jungle and attacked her pursuers.

The girl ran a little further before collapsing on the road. The men tried to get back to the girl, but the lions lay down in the road, keeping watch over the child. For several hours, the giant cats stood guard until a police car arrived and picked her up off the road, taking her to safety. Several of her captors were later arrested.

Word travelled fast around the world about the incident. A local official told the press that people were calling it a miracle.

As for the lions, they simply went back into the jungle, never to be seen again. As Amos states, "The lion has roared—who will not fear? The Sovereign LORD has spoken—who can but prophesy?"[313]

Down through history, names have been used to signify more than a person's identity, they would be used to describe someone's character and destiny. For centuries it was believed that if one could know the name of a demon or a god, one could then control that entity.

Today people often try to fulfill their need for significance by creating unique ways to spell their children's names, others have resorted to calling their newborns by titles and adjectives such as *king* or *beautiful*. Numerous people have taken the name Abcde, and at least one person has successfully changed their name to all 26 letters of the alphabet.

Then there is the practice of some entertainers who have replaced letters in their names with symbols to distinguish themselves in the market. Other wealthy artists have foisted on their children names of fictional characters from other planets, or produced names by combining words that make little sense.

It is rare to meet anyone named Hitler, nor will you or I likely meet someone named Judas; and while the most common name in the world is Muhammad, there is little agreement on how it should be spelled. And when the angel declared to a frightened Joseph, "You are to give him the name Jesus,"[314] it wasn't because it was a common name so he could be identified with everyday people as some have taught.

Often names were changed to signify a new identity. Perhaps, the most dramatic was a man named *Jacob*, a word that meant "heal grabber" or "one who trips another," signifying one who was dishonest. Jacob spent much of his life swindling others, so much so that his brother lamented, "Isn't his name rightly called Jacob?"³¹⁵ However, after a life changing encounter with God, he was left humbled and transformed. It was then he was renamed *Israel*, "one who sees God."³¹⁶

One of the most important names to be changed was that of *Abram*, a word that meant "father," to *Abraham*, which carries the meaning of "father of multitudes."³¹⁷ Abraham was the first man to radically believe the promises of God and share them with the world, thus he is considered the spiritual parent of many.

Far less known in history is the name of a man named Hoshea found in the Old Testament. In the Hebrew Bible, Moses is a daunting figure whose life was used to lead and deliver a nation. Though his story is vast, there is one moment that is often overlooked.

Hoshea was a student of the great leader, and when Moses gave his soon-to-be successor an instruction to follow, he first changed his name. In a subtle statement we are simply told, "Moses gave Hoshea son of Nun the name Joshua."³¹⁸

As history tells us, Moses did not conquer the Promised Land, Joshua did. While Moses received divine laws and taught the people how to live as a community of faith, it was Joshua who would lead a new generation victoriously into Canaan, and it is his new name that is of particular interest.

For various reasons, most of them due to supposed taboos in different cultures, multiple translators of scripture have opted to use the title *God* for the divine name of the creator revealed and recorded some 7000 times in the Old Testament, *YHWH*.³¹⁹ Some English versions opt to use "I am that I am" in lieu of writing the letters YHWH; others instead record the word LORD in all capital letters to signify the divine name. For one of *thousands* of examples, consider the well-known account of Hagar's prayer in the Genesis 16:13. The King James translators chose the nonspecific which reads, "And she called the name of the Lord that spake unto her, Thou God seest me." Compare the literal translation of *The Sacred Scriptures: Bethel Edition*; "And she called the name of Yahweh that spoke unto her, You are an El that sees." Likewise *The Jerusalem Bible* records, "Hagar gave a name to Yahweh who had spoke to her: 'You are El Roi.'"

Ross notes, "The name is crucial in biblical theology. God's personal name is Yahweh...in Israel a name represents the whole person and thus becomes a powerful force, as powerful as the person named. A name could be blotted out, redeemed, praised, prayed to, preserved for an inheritance, made famous, win battles, or dwell among individuals. The 'name of the LORD' is clearly a force to be reckoned with in the Old Testament because it represents the divine nature, all that God is known to be."[320]

Translators opting to use titles such as *God* or *LORD* in various versions means incredibly important meanings behind name structures are missed by readers.

The name *Joshua* is literally "*Yahweh saves.*" While Moses represented the laws of right living and man's responsibilities of justice and mercy, in his own strength, man is unable to reach the Promised Land, which is why Moses could not take the people there. Humanity needs divine assistance; thus, Joshua would lead the people into their inheritance.

Fifteen centuries later, a young couple were told to name their child Jesus, which is simply the Greek form of the name Joshua. Jesus was not given his name because it was common, he was given his name to display his destiny; "Yahweh saves." It was his mission to bring deliverance from sin, death, and the evil one. What people could never do, Christ, *Yahweh saves*, did for us. Such is why in heaven it is declared of him, "Behold, the Lion of the tribe of Judah!"

Moses, representing the law or religion, cannot save, because no one can claim to have perfectly kept the commandments. Each person has at many times been a "law breaker," thus each person is left guilty before the law. Therefore, only with divine help of a perfect advocate, the *new* Joshua, could people by redeemed. Since Jesus never broke the commandments, his record is clear. He offers to trade his spotless record for our tainted one, so we can be avowed "not guilty" before the law. It is not human effort, but by divine grace by which we are saved.

The question is, saved from *what*, and *to what*? Answering and understanding that will help us go a long way in understanding why *each of us* will eventually be given a new and mysterious name by God.[321] (See the upcoming discussion on *sozo* for a fuller answer to this question.)

First, consider another man with an interesting name. His story is found in a simple clause in the Gospel of John which reads, "Judas (not Iscariot), said unto him, 'Lord, how is it that you will manifest yourself?'"[322] To distinguish this person from the infamous traitor, he was known as Judas, "but not *that* Judas." Imagine having to continually carry around the stigma of explaining your identity.

However, this Judas had another name as well; he was called Thaddaeus, and later Judas Thaddaeus, and then simply *Jude*. Because of his faith, he became identified with impossible things, which is one of the reasons St. Jude Children's Hospital took his name.

While not much is known of Thaddeus, history tells us he was chosen as one of the original disciples of Jesus, and later died for his faith. His old name did not hold him back, no matter how many stigmas it held, rather he went on to be a force for good, and two thousand years later one of the most well-known medical institutes in the world uses his name to designate their belief in overcoming any obstacle.

Just as his story ends with triumph, so can yours, as you are not your past, and you can find a new and powerful identity in a moment of decision.

Years ago, Sylvester Stallone wanted to be an actor, but after over *1000* rejections by directors and producers, most people would have long since given up. When his dream seemed to be far out of reach, with little support from anyone else and running out of money, he had to sell his dog to pay the bills. It was rock bottom.

Then he witnessed a boxing match on television, where after taking a brutal beating one boxer heroically kept picking himself up off the canvas to continue to fight. That night he was inspired to write the script for *Rocky*.

He was offered $100,000 for the story, but turned it down when the studio wanted someone else to play the lead role. Finally, a director agreed to cast him as Rocky, a role for which he later won an Oscar. Before the movie wrapped, he was able to find his dog and buy him back,[323] a story that powerfully illustrates what happens when a person refuses to give up.

As you make a new beginning, you may find it helpful to come up with a nickname for yourself or to start going by your middle name as a way to express your fresh start. Another helpful tool to strengthen your identity is to include an emotional word as part of your password so every time you sign in to an account you type a reminder of your higher aspirations with a power word such as *love, passion, strength, confident, fitness, skinny* or *wealth*. Tom Oliver suggests writing the number 1 on your palm each day as a visual anchor to remind yourself to focus of your main goal.[324] A ring or a bracelet or watch can also be a trigger to help you remember to focus on first things first.

Personally, I have a number of images of David defeating Goliath around my home, especially where I do research and writing. I also have several Marine Corps emblems on my walls as well as one on my ring to remind me to keep a higher standard for myself, as well as a way to reflect on accomplishments from my time in the military where we pushed ourselves physically and mentally beyond endurance. It is following the rule that, "Confidence begets confidence."[325] (In the final chapter, we will visit one of the absolutely most powerful psychological tools for making change you will find anywhere.)

It is important to understand that making a change in one area can have a profound influence on every aspect of your life. This message is part of the concept the gospels portray. Take for a moment the word found in the New Testament translated as *saved* or *salvation*. In Greek it is *sozo*, and it is a term filled with meaning. The same word is also used for *wholeness* and *healing*.[326] It means to deliver, to protect, and entails "a complete work of making a person whole in spirit, soul, and body."[327]

There is a deliverance *from* sin, but there is also a deliverance *to* a whole new way of victorious living. Jesus called it abundant life, or to "have life, and have it to the full."[328] While he gave his life to set people free from sin and the fear of death, he also empowers us to live in the "now" triumphantly.

I always tell people that when Jesus talked about bearing your cross,[329] he was not talking about your mother-in-law. He was talking about what Watchman Nee referred to as the "exchanged life," and about what Norman Grubb called the "replaced life."[330]

To take up your cross means to recognize the death of your old self and way of living, and to embrace a new life in which you know and experience "this mystery, which is Christ in you, the hope of glory."[331]

Ole Anthony states, "When you are forgotten, or neglected, or purposely provoked, and you don't sting and hurt with the insult or the oversight, but your heart is happy, being counted worthy to suffer for Christ—that is dying to self."[332]

I remember when I drove one of those cars that you had to go through a checklist to start. When people would ask to borrow it I would have to prep them before they could take the driver's seat.

"Okay, when you turn the key it won't start, but it is getting ready to. So let off the ignition for four seconds, then put the gas pedal to the floor and crank the key and it should turn over right away. If it doesn't you will have to pump the pedal three times, then repeat the steps above as needed. *Oh*, and when you come to a stop light put it in neutral and keep the gas pedal pressed down, you don't want to stall this thing or it won't start again until next Tuesday!"

It is not that I didn't want people to borrow the car; it was just... complicated.

I feel the same way when talking to individuals who question why some people who say they love God are so unkind. I often find myself trying to clarify, "Well, you see, there is the religion of Christianity, and then there is being a Christian, and they aren't the same thing. And there are lots of people who attend *church*, but that is different than realizing that in the 1st Century that word was used to describe a 'called-out' group of people, and not a building." I often just receive blank stares. You see, it is complicated.

Then there are our own lives. There are bills to be paid, jobs to be done, people pulling is in many different directions. Others are caught on the exhausting wheel of religion, convinced that if they somehow work hard enough at being "good," they will be more acceptable. Yet the Apostle Paul, one of the most religious people of all time, warned that being very religious in his own life had added up to "a loss" and to "garbage," or as the King James translates his words, *dung*.[333] The truth he said, was found in one who had been buried in a borrowed tomb, but had long since left the grave behind.

A philosopher once asked, "I have only two questions: has anyone ever beaten death, and has he made a way for me to do it?" And we realize the answer is Jesus, but we also know for many it just is not that simple. Research shows that most people believe Jesus resurrected; they just need others to help them understand why that matters to their life.

Many grew up with parents who denied their own need to answer the big questions because someone squashed that desire inside. These selfsame parents denied their own hearts, and learned to keep quiet. When people feel that life is unsafe, they tend to stay guarded and learn to conform. Young people enter school with defense systems in place, ready to not look foolish; cynical and untrusting they learn to *hide*. Students tease others to reinforce their own insecurities. The cycle continues even as we grow older.[334]

We ignore the core of ourselves, afraid of what people will think, keeping our feelings buried deep inside, seeking love but withholding self from receiving it. The price can be enormous. Everyone faces it, and so many deny it, and stay wounded. Then we learn not to expect much. And trust? Trust, in a time like today?

As a nation and as a culture, we continue to drift off course. Just over fifty years ago, 39 million students and more than 2 million teachers were barred from opening the day in public schools with a simple prayer; "Almighty God, we acknowledge our dependence upon Thee, and we beg Thy blessings upon us, our parents, our teachers and our country."[335]

In the late 1960s, things continued to go off the rails at an alarming rate. A few short years after the Kennedy assassinations, the Manson Family committed the Tate-LaBianca murders. It was the tragic end of the decade of *do what thou wilt*. The day after Manson's grand jury hearing, the Rolling Stones gave a concert for which they hired the Hell's Angels as bodyguards. The biker gang infamously killed a man as the Stones played "Sympathy for the Devil."[336] The season of "peace and love" was over.

A few months later, Jim Morrison of the Doors died mysteriously in Paris. Shortly before his death, he paraded around like a messiah on stage, holding a lamb to his chest. He claimed he was possessed, eventually marrying a Wiccan priestess and drinking blood. He was 27 when he passed away.[337]

Shortly before he was gunned down, John Lennon gave a final interview in which he stated, "There is no one answer to anything."[338] He had spent months visiting psychics and attending séances, finding little hope to hold onto. His death would be preceded by Elvis's, who succumbed to an apparent overdose and asphyxiation after severe abuse of food and drugs. All of this was simply a prelude to the 1970s, the decade of divorce. It would seem that year after year, things have only become more chaotic.

We need to begin putting our trust in one who is immovable. Because he lives, everything has changed. Like the psalmist who cried, "Lead me to the rock that is higher than I,"[339] it is essential we find the foundation that will stand in these turbulent times. Part of that means surrounding the old self to the cross, and fully embracing the work of *sozo*, recognizing that we "can do all things through Christ which strengtheneth."[340] He saved us from darkness to bring us into the light so that we can be a witness to him doing his work in us. Our job is to rest in the promises he has made, and teach others in word and in deed how they can do the same. In the end, perhaps some things are not so complicated after all.

CHAPTER 9

BEYOND BELIEF

"I used to ask God to help me. Then I asked God if I could help Him. Finally I ended up asking God to do His work through me."

– Hudson Taylor

Johnny Cash recorded more than 1500 songs, selling 15 million albums. His life was a major influence on Elvis, as well as countless other musicians. Unfortunately, he began taking drugs, something he would do for ten years. He would go on to share that getting high increased his energy and gave him confidence and connection. He would lament that no matter how many drugs he consumed, he was never able to reach the initial rush of the first time. His addiction slowly began to rip his world apart.

Often, Cash took handfuls of pills to ease his pain. Over the years, he spent time in jail for various offenses, and more than once, he wrecked cars and lives around him because of his habit. Finally after having lost all hope, he took a flashlight into a cave and crawled for hours until the batteries went dead, leaving himself in pitch black. Then he lay down and waited to die. His plan was simple: crawl so far into the cave no one would be able to rescue him.

In the pitch black, unable to save himself, he shared that in the darkness, God powerfully visited him, and he realized his life was not his own. He considered it a miracle that he was able to crawl out of the cave unharmed in total darkness. When he reached the exit of the cavern, June Carter and his mom were there, having driven from California to Tennessee because they knew something was wrong. He and June were together for the next 35 years.

Cash later shared about that night in the cave, "The absolute lack of light was appropriate, for at that moment, I was as far from God as I have ever been. My separation from Him, the deepest and most ravaging of the various kinds of loneliness I'd felt over the years, seemed finally complete."[341]

Cash wore black the rest of his life to identify with hurting people, especially those in jail. His fervor and passion for God and people led him to write many songs of hope, and even to work with Billy Graham. It wasn't the drugs or the alcohol, but the kingdom within that changed his whole life.

As Jesus stated, "The kingdom of God does not come with your careful observation, nor will people say, 'Here it is,' or 'There it is,' because the kingdom of God is within you."[342]

The mystery of the kingdom is not in religion or in a building or in a program; it is in you. It is not in regulating the type of music someone listens to, judging what political party a person agree with, or in any list of do's and don'ts. The kingdom is a supernatural work apart from human effort because of the mystery revealed in Christ.

You are now a vessel of God, containing a Person. Over 200 times, scripture uses the term *in Christ*, with three quarters of those referring "directly to the fact that Christ, the Word, is the life of the believer."[343] As Paul would share: "God has chosen to make known among the Gentiles the glorious riches of this mystery, which is *Christ in you, the hope of glory.*"³⁴⁴

In light of this, a century ago, A. J. Gordon wrote, "We have authority to take from the enemy everything he is holding back. The chief way of taking is by prayer, and by whatever action prayer leads us to. The cry that should be ringing out today is the great cry, 'Take, in Jesus' Great Name!'"

The apostle faced accusers who feared that if people understood the concept of grace and forgiveness he taught, they would then do as they please. Paul responded, "Shall we go on sinning so that grace may increase?"³⁴⁵ Anticipating further arguments of men who would selfishly take the grace of God for granted, Paul asks the question before his detractors can, *if God is glorified by me being forgiven, then should I sin more so his forgiveness comes more often?* He would answer, "We died to sin; how can we live in it any longer?"³⁴⁶

His point was simply that if someone takes lightly the sacrifice Jesus made and uses that gift as a license to sin, then they have no concept of the grace Jesus offers, nor of what it truly cost him. On the contrary, as we recognize the mystery more and more, we crawl out of the darkness, not further into it. When we understand Christ is now within us, our lives are radically transformed. Grace makes us better people, not worse; it brings us closer to Jesus, not further away.

In life, what we focus on is what we feel. While the subconscious mind sorts through at least 2 *billion* pieces of data every second, we can consciously only pay attention to roughly half a dozen bits of that information.³⁴⁷ Hall and Belnap note that as "we handle the billions of bytes of information per second striking our nervous system, we delete most of this information, generalize a good bit of it, and distort the rest of it."[348] We often delete the positives and more easily remember the negative moments. However, there is a way to change this.

In the brain, the reticular activating system (RAS) filters out what it believes is unimportant information, so you have to consciously decide what is important, and then train your brain to stop filtering it out by learning to control your thinking and the meanings you assign to events in life.

For instance, every day, you drive by dozens of businesses, but you don't notice them unless you are specifically looking for a certain company. You have directed your brain (RAS) to be on the lookout for a particular building, which is why you see it when you drive down the road. This is also what happens when we experience the interesting phenomena of buying a new car and suddenly noticing the same model on every street corner. The vehicles were always on the road; your brain just didn't consciously pay attention to them because you never directed it to do so.

Part of the gift of humanity is being able to direct our thinking, and through repetition training our brain as to what to notice. This is one reason writing down goals is so important, it is directing your mind to pay attention to certain stimulus. Mostly, the RAS deletes information from our thoughts. For example, we don't feel the shoes on our feet unless someone reminds us to notice them. So, if you want to change the way you feel, change what you focus on moment to moment.

If you have a religion that tells you to focus on feeling guilty, then you will run that program. If you believe life is filled with pain, you will find yourself constantly directing your attention to painful things. But what if you focused on possibilities, on love, and on complete and utter forgiveness and grace? What if you noticed more and more what it means to be declared *not guilty* in the courts of heaven?

Rituals make or break us; repetition can either chain us or set us free. When a person rehearses fear and judgment and doubt, they are feeding those very emotions and training their brain to find those traits in other people and in day to day experiences. If a person focuses upon their sin in an attempt to *not* commit that particular transgression, they are filling their mind with what they don't want, which will produce the opposite result they truly desire. The very sin they are wishing to avoid consumes their thinking as they create an unending loop, *focus, fear, sin, guilt, repeat*. This is one reason willpower produces limited results, there is already a long chain of thinking under the radar that is directing our brain.

If instead of focusing upon sin and guilt a person chose to focus upon grace, the resurrection, and the life of Jesus and how to be more conformed to his image, they would be feeding their core to notice a completely different type of life. Again, our lives are either an example or a warning. Chuck Colson said, "Rather than cursing the darkness, we need to be lighting a candle."[349]

After studying various cultures around the world and down through history, C.S. Lewis stated, "Think of a country where people were admired for running away from battle, or where a man felt proud of double-crossing all the people who had been kindest to him...Selfishness has never been admired."[350]

For Lewis, this universal internal moral law helped him to believe there was a law giver, leading him from atheism to faith in God. Selfishness is never admired, so rather than take the grace of Jesus for granted how much more powerful and useful it would be to focus our minds on the gift he has given. If we can see the beauty of his sacrifice we will recognize that his life has entered ours and we are dead to sin, so we will live more and more to him and less and less to self and sin.

Scientists tell us that koalas sleep twenty-two hours a day, blissfully drugged out on eucalyptus plants. Mayflies live only twenty-four hours. In like manner, how many people are caught in a daily slumber, oblivious to world around them? What would you do differently if you knew you only had a day left?

In nature, spiders produce three different types of silk, creating sixty feet of it in one hour, while creating a special oil for their feet so they don't stick to their own web.[351] Light travels around the earth over seven times in *one second*. The golden plover migrates 8,000 miles annually, including navigating over 2,000 miles of sea. Similarly, the barn swallow travels 9,000 miles, while the arctic tern navigates 14,000 miles a year.[352] Three hundred years ago, Jonathan Edwards shared, "Nature is God's greatest evangelist." Nature cries out to humanity so hurriedly moving along to simply stop and notice. It is embracing what Colin Wilson called "magic moments" where we have a "sense of the marvelous *interestingness* of the world."[353]

So many are saturating and distracting themselves with shopping and busyness and self-seeking as they miss the evidence of God around them. Martin Luther called this selling our birthright for a pot of soup. Internally, we all know that things are not as they are supposed to be. And the kingdom of God? Our Savior told us to not look externally for it, but rather inside. The mystery that was hidden for ages has now been revealed: *Christ in you, the hope of glory*.[354]

The story of the prodigal son tells of a man who squanders his father's inheritance on wild living until he finds himself homeless and destitute. In the story, we are told at his lowest point, he "came to his senses."[355] The language here could read that he got his *sanity* back. Once the insanity of sin lost its pull, he was able to seek help from his father who saw him off in the distance and *ran*[356] to embrace him, welcoming him back home.

When I was an undergrad, a speaker named Steve offered the following illustration. He shared that one day, he was at the hospital when he was asked to visit a woman who had been sexually abused several times by various people. She found herself in the psychiatric ward unable to cope any longer, ready to commit suicide. Steve agreed to try and help her, but found her unresponsive in her room, just blankly staring at the wall.

He sat down and talked with her for about an hour, telling her about his life and family. The entire time, she refused to acknowledge his presence, just staring at the wall in front of her. Finally, he got up to leave, telling her that maybe he would see her again. As he reached the door, she spoke for the first time, "Why don't you want to kill yourself like I want to kill myself?"

Thinking for a moment, Steve replied, "Because he lives, I can face tomorrow." Sensing a breakthrough, he agreed to come back later that week. Before long, she put her faith in Christ as Steve and a number of faithful believers came to visit her. Within weeks, she was released from the hospital, completely transformed.

After a couple years, she moved away. One day, she wrote to Steve and told him, "I tree you." She was getting married and requested he and his wife attend her wedding. They gladly attended, inspired by the remarkable transformation in her life. After the reception, he asked her what she meant when she ended her letters, "I tree you."

She began to recall the hurt in her life, the pain of betrayal and abuse by people who were supposed to love her. "People too easily say 'I love you.' The ones who said it to me were the ones who hurt me the most. I don't know what love is, but I know that trees are beautiful. That is something I can relate to, so I end all my letters that way." Then pausing, she said, "Are there any trees in the Bible?"

Steve looked her in the eye and said, "There is the most amazing tree in the Bible, one on which Jesus died for the sins of the world, that we might know the life he brings."

How far does God go to gain our attention, to show us that he is on our side, waiting for our complete surrender? King David was one of the heroes of history, leading a nation from a faith based heart. He displayed a passion for God, a dedication to personal holiness, and a commitment to defend his people that few have rivalled.

When King Saul turned against him and tried to violently destroy him, David chose to leave the city rather than shed blood against his king. Saul had become insanely jealous of David who the people deeply loved for defeating Goliath. Later when he was told David was the rightful heir to the throne, Saul could no longer control his rage. On at least two occasions he tried to pin the young giant slayer to the wall with a spear.

Rather than continue to ignore the attacks of the king or go to war for his royal seat, David chose to leave the city. In the process of keeping the peace, he had to say goodbye to his closest friend Jonathan, Saul's son.

David's first stop as a fugitive was the temple. David asked one of the nervous priests for food. The priest told him, "I only have some holy bread here."[357] He was talking about the loaves that were made daily in the Temple, which were reserved for the priests. David was born in Bethlehem, literally "the house of bread." It was from this same town that the Mary would give birth to the Messiah. Jesus would later say of himself, "I am the bread of life."³⁵⁸ When David needed sustenance, a voice whispered, *there is only holy bread here.*

Next David asked for a weapon. Tellingly the priest responds, "The sword of Goliath, the Philistine, is here...If you want it, take it. *It's the only sword here.*"³⁵⁹ When David needed a weapon there was only the one carried by his greatest opponent who he successfully defeated on the battlefield. *Take the bread, take the sword...remember who you are* a voice whispered.

David then fled to another city. Some of the people recognized him even though he tried to hide his identity. The people began to recite the song made in his honor not so long ago to celebrate his military victories, "Saul has killed thousands of men. David has killed tens of thousands."³⁶⁰

First, it was the holy bread, then it was the sword of victory, and as a final reminder of his destiny, the people began to sing a song; all reminding David of God's presence and his calling. His destiny was to be king; he may have forgotten that in his struggles with Saul, but God never did. So God sent messages to remind him, to encourage him. Like mile markers on his path, signs kept pointing him back to this one truth, he was never alone. And because of that, David had nothing to fear. *The kingdom of heaven lies within.* As Anthony Robbins shares, "I believe life is always happening for us, not to us!"³⁶¹

Author Ron Auch wrote very candidly about his struggles to be faithful to his wife. After infidelity almost destroyed his marriage, he committed to growing his faith and became a changed man. He began to seek to rebuild trust in their relationship, but after many months he felt he was making little progress with his wife. Finally, in desperation, he prayed and asked God when he would give him his wife back. Immediately he felt heaven's reply in his heart, "Just as soon as you give Me yourself."³⁶²

There are many moments, if we will but train our minds to notice them, of God pulling us back to himself, wooing us to fully commit to his calling to fulfill our destiny of being conformed to live like Jesus. At the same time there is nothing wrong with admitting there are mysteries we simply do not comprehend about life and faith. As Sherri Gragg stated, "Jesus can handle your doubt."

In fact, times of doubt are often part of the growth process we need as the flame of a candle is easier to see in the dark. Even Mother Teresa expressed moments of feeling distant from God, telling a mentor, "Jesus has a very special love for you. As for me, the silence and the emptiness is so great I look and do not see, listen and do not hear."[363] Yet, it was in those times she grew spiritual muscle that allowed her to attend to the deeper needs of those under her care.

As the psalmist's words pour off the page, we read of God's presence, "If I go up to the heavens, you are there; if I make my bed in the depths, you are there."[364] David needed reminders of that, and so do you and I. All around us are the signposts of God's grace, if we but pay attention a little more closely. Instead of falling for the materialistic trap of believing that life is a series of random, meaningless events, how much better like David to recognize and fully embrace from the core of our being that "what happens to you happens for you."[365]

As we direct our brain to notice more love, more forgiveness, more of the things that truly produce success and happiness, we will begin to more clearly see that it is grace alone which will bring us from the darkness and into the light. And if we pay attention and listen, we can hear the still small voice whisper, *Never will I leave you; never will I forsake you.*[366]

CHAPTER 10

A NEW LIFE

"Our chief want in life is somebody who shall make us what we can be."

– **Ralph Waldo Emerson**

It was Karl Marx who said, "Religion is the opium of the people." As an atheist he believed man should focus only on the here and now, especially addressing what he deemed was the greatest injustice, the division of social classes. He sought to convince the masses that the rich had invented religion as a tool of oppression; therefore religion was the enemy of mankind.

Marx believed man had the ability to fix every problem in the world without the need of divine assistance. But for all his "answers," Marx lived and died broke and depressed. He lived in such poverty that when his son died, his wife had to beg on the street for someone to pay for the funeral.[367] Sadly, Marx never saw past man-made religious systems to see there was something far different being offered.

Then there was the World War I ambulance driver. Born in 1899, he came to be known as Papa. Being almost killed by a mortar and watching his fellow soldiers die left him deeply scarred.

Oddly, his own life would continue to be marked by several close calls with death, including two plane crashes that left him severely injured.

Eventually, Papa moved to Paris to become a better writer, focusing on his craft and upon feeding his every whim. He indulged in pleasure with vigor, and in the process, he concluded that faith in God was a waste of time. While his wild living ruined his health, he would also become a tortured artist, mainly fighting what would prove to be a losing battle with depression. As he began to age, he lamented the loss of his health and of his friends, and bemoaned his lonely estate, failing to find fulfillment in his numerous marital affairs. Key to his pain was his sick mother, who one year, mailed him a birthday cake and the gun his father killed himself with.

To Papa, life had simply become chaotic. It was from the final frontier that he was determined to take back control. With precision, he began to plot his own death. His opportunity came one early morning. Dressed in a robe, he locked himself in a room with a shotgun and ended his own life, a final effort to be captain of his own fate, a desperate attempt to take control of something. Though a legendary writer, Ernest Hemingway is perhaps most often remembered for his untimely death; the tortured artist was truly a tortured soul. What is so puzzling to many people is how a man who seemed to have so much could have felt so empty inside.[368]

Contrast his story with that of W. Mitchell, who riding home one night on his motorcycle, found himself face to face with a Mack truck. Mitchell laid down his bike in an effort to avoid colliding with the trailer, but as his bike skidded across the pavement, the gas cap popped off, causing sparks to ignite the ground and his body in flames. Refusing to give up on his dreams, though badly burned on over 75% of his body, Mitchell eventually learned to fly airplanes. Incomprehensibly on one fateful flight, an emergency landing left him paralyzed from the waist down.[369]

For Hemingway, adoring fans, a successful career and a family could not quiet the demons that haunted him. In contrast, though burns cover three-quarters of his body, W. Mitchell lives a life of happiness and humor, even once having run for congress with the slogan, "Send me to Congress, and I won't be just another pretty face." He became wildly successful in business, married the woman of his dreams, and has been an inspiration to countless men and women. As he shares, "Before I was paralyzed, there were 10,000 things I could do; now there are 9,000. I can either dwell on the 1,000 I've lost or focus on the 9,000 I have left."[370]

In Britain, Steve Cunningham inspires countless people to this day. Having lost his eyesight, he became the first blind man to fly a plane, race a car, race a boat, and captain the English football team.[371] With faith and focus and a completely different way of thinking, life takes on new dimensions, and entire cities can be changed.

For some three hundred years, the early church suffered persecution in the form of many martyrs. Countless men and women were crucified, a practice that was finally banned by Constantine in AD 325. However, Rome replaced the martyrs with gladiators, drawing the same bloodthirsty crowds to the arenas that had previously watched public executions.

Around AD 400, a monk named Telemachus walked into the stadium where two gladiators were fighting to the death. Climbing into the arena he placed his hands upon the men and pleaded with them to stop the violence. Angry, the crowd and Roman prefect called for the execution of the monk. The gladiators struck him down to the pleasure of a cheering crowd.

As his breath left him and the monk died, the cheers died down as well. The people realized how grotesque their games were and how far they had fallen. The bloodthirsty crowd was now caught up in remorse, as were the fighters. It was the monk's death that would lead to the banning of the gladiator games.[372]

No matter how dark things are, the light always overcomes. The light is not a religion, but rather a person, the divine fully expressed in Jesus. When people ask, "What is God like?" The scriptures point to Christ and tell us, *behold*.[373]

People in the 1st Century were familiar with stories of healers. However, as Dr. Ron Moseley notes, what Jesus did was far beyond what anyone else had ever seen or heard.[374] He was not only able to heal one leper, something most people did not believe possible; he healed *ten* at a time.[375] He then cast a demon out of mute man when people believed deliverance was only possible when they could garner the name of the evil spirit from the victim.[376] The crowds were so stunned when they witnessed this they proclaimed, "Nothing like this has ever been seen in Israel."[377] Third, he healed a man born blind, something so unheard of even the crowds could not stop talking about; causing the Pharisees to question the man and his parents if they were sure he had been born this way because, "Nobody has ever heard of opening the eyes of a man born blind."[378] Lastly, he raised Lazarus after *four* days in a culture where people believed resurrection was not possible after the third day as it was believed the soul departed the earth after 72 hours.[379] This event so rattled the nation John says the religious leaders "from that day on plotted to take his life."[380] Four unheard of miracles, all done to point people to the desired of all nations.[381] How far will the Savior go to get our attention? The evidence is ever before us, if only we choose to see.

One of the strangest cases of mass hysteria happened in seventeenth century Poland. Tulips had become a symbol of the rich, with people vying for certain colors of the seemingly rare flower. Things began innocently enough, with buyers competing for the healthiest bulbs, paying hundreds of dollars for a single one.

But as sales continued to rise, the Amsterdam stock exchange began to trade the flowers, and the demand for tulips continued to grow at an alarming rate. Before long people began to invest their entire savings in the flower. A certain madness had truly set in.

Finally, the government stepped in to bring an end to the tulip craze by regulating sales. In a matter of days, the flower lost all economic value, and everyone who had one tried desperately to make a final sale. But it was too late; people that had mortgaged their home for a single flower ended up out on the street, worthless bulb in hand.[382]

George Santayana famously said, "Those who cannot remember the past are condemned to repeat it." Yet, how often do we find ourselves caught up in the fad of the day, or distracting ourselves with "entertainment" that leaves us dull in mind and heart?

As someone has written;

Don't look—you might see.
Don't listen—you might hear.
Don't think—you might learn.
Don't make a decision—you might be wrong.
Don't walk—you might stumble.
Don't run—you might fall.
Don't live—you might die.

One of the challenges to making lasting change is there is little consequence to not keepings one's word. When someone promises to stop smoking but fails to follow through, no one is surprised. If a colleague says they are going to get in shape but are caught eating donuts in the breakroom, coworkers just laugh it off and say, "Oh well, you can start that diet tomorrow." Resolutions made on the first day of the year are known to be broken by the third week of January.

It is the same for many spiritual and character commitments. Far too many know the pain of people that promise to make a change simply returning to their old ways; husbands that commit to being more loving, mothers that vow to pay more attention, leaders that say it is a new day. Paul would state the problem, "I do not understand what I do. For what I want to do I do not do, but what I hate I do."[383]

There is a system of motivation that works, but only for those who are truly ready to make a change, no matter the cost. As previously stated, money provides little motivation for employees, however accountability and paying a high price for failure will motivate even the laziest person.

Here are the mechanics of this strategy, whether you are ready to follow a gym plan, become a person of integrity, raise your standards as a spouse, turn from a certain sin, or any other thing. The answer is simple, when the consequence is great enough, people will change. We have to be the ones to hold ourselves to this level of commitment, providing accountability when we fail to do what we said we would. As Moses would caution, "be careful to perform what goes out from your lips."[384]

Using the gym as an example, first sign a letter of commitment with someone who will hold you to your word. Let's say you commit to working out three days a week. Next, give the other person five checks, each for $100. Promise to text or call them at the end of the week and simply say you kept your commitment, or you didn't, and for every day you failed to follow through, the other person gets $100. Now, failing to follow through doesn't simply mean going back on your word; if you stay in bed instead of hitting the gym, it will cost you $100 every time.

For another example, take someone who loses their temper. Every time they fail to control their words or their emotions, they must confess to their accountability partner who will cash their checks. Want to gain even more leverage on yourself? Address several envelopes to a person you don't like, with money inside. When you fail to keep your promises, drop the letter in the mailbox.

Will this work the first time? Perhaps not, but after constantly paying $100 for your next cigarette or temper tantrum, the lesson will quickly sink in. Sending money to your ex when you blow your stack will quickly get old, and your brain will finally get the picture: *acting like this is too painful, too costly, so let's find another answer.*

In the Marine Corps, it was common to gain leverage with this type of procedure because it works. Lazy recruits were not rewarded by getting off the hook. The rest of the platoon was punished for this individual's choices by having to run further and do more pushups. When a private could see the real cost of their failure, what it did to others around them, suddenly they learned to come through even when they didn't feel like it.

It is the same for you and me. When your ex calls and asks why they just received $100 in the mail and you have to say, "Because I broke a promise," you will literally think long and hard about not keeping your word the next time.

Milton Erickson talked about making it harder to keep the problem than to let it go. He as well proposed making it more painful to continue to the unwanted behavior than to give it up.

He suggested that if a person has an emotion or behavior that continues to show up when they want to move beyond it, on those days where the problem persists, contract with yourself to get up at two in the morning to exercise.[385] Once the consequences are uncomfortable enough, change will happen.

Is your marriage worth fighting for? What is the value of your integrity? Are you willing to pay the price of making lasting change, no matter what it costs? Then be willing to do whatever it takes.

For people like Marx, what caused so much doubt was often the little difference they saw in people that claimed to be believers. When a nation was confronted by a man of high character like Telemachus, it changed its entire laws.

Scripture encourages people to pursue holiness, "without which no man shall see the Lord."[386] It is important to remember that personal change is not just a mental activity. It has to be something from our heart that transitions into action and doing the work to live apart from sin and selfishness.

We live in a world that is facing tremendous confusion and compromise in the area of morality. The New Testament has harsh criticism for Esau who famously gave up his birthright for food, labelling him as "godless...who for a single meal sold his inheritance rights as the oldest son."[387] *Godless*! Some translations have *unspiritual, immoral,* and even *unholy*. The word contains the idea of being accessible to all, having zero personal standards.

It is no small matter to be a hypocrite, to take the cross of Christ lightly, and to live in a way that mocks the very faith men and women have died for. People who trade their integrity for a bowl of soup in the moment are losing more than they can imagine. Luther himself would say he only had two days on his calendar: "today" and "that Day" on which he would give an account for his life.[388]

Did you ever wonder what happened to the disciples? Once they grasped the gift they had received this rag tag band of men became world changers, pouring their lives out in love and gratitude. History tells us they all, with the exception of John, met their end as martyrs:

- Philip—crucified
- Andrew—crucified
- Jude—crucified
- Bartholomew—crucified
- Simon—crucified
- Peter—crucified (tradition says upside down.)
- Matthew—speared in Ethiopia
- James (1/2 brother to Jesus)—thrown from the Temple and stoned
- Thomas—speared in India
- James (brother of John)—beheaded
- Matthias (who replaced Judas)—beheaded
- Mark—burned to death
- Luke—hung on a tree
- John—boiled in oil (survived, only to be imprisoned on an island)
- Paul—beheaded the same day Peter was crucified

What a difference to know this mystery, Christ in you, the hope of glory, and to be able to face life without fear.[389]

It is said that that Leonardo da Vinci had a falling out with a friend before he painted The Last Supper. He then determined to paint his newfound enemy as Judas. When he finished it was what he imagined was the perfect likeness. However, he then struggled to paint the face of Jesus, unable to create what he wanted. He realized his bitterness had entrapped him.

After he changed the face of Judas, no longer making it that of his former friend, he then found it easy to paint the face of Christ, free from the chains of anger that kept him from completing his masterpiece. When we can see that for freedom we have been set free, we behold Christ more clearly in our life, and then we can breathe in his grace.

There is a humorous story of a man who was shipwrecked on an island. Finally, after five years, a boat sails close enough to see his smoke signal. When the rescue boat arrives to pick him up, he quickly gathers his things. However, the captain notices three huts on the shore.

As the man gets into the boat, the captain asks, "Are you alone on this island?"

The man replies, "Yes, of course."

Confused, the captain asks, "Then why are there three huts?"

Without skipping a beat, the man answers, "That hut is my house, and that hut is where I go to church."

"And the third one?" the captain asks.

The man responds, "Oh that? That is where I *used* to go to church!"

We often act so small because we focus only on small things, holding grudges and resentments, belittling other people in the process. In contrast, an ancient teaching suggests that a legion of angels goes before each human proclaiming, "Behold, the image of God!" How much different we respond to the demands of life when we move beyond the petty to the eternal and see people with the mind of Christ.

Nigerian minister D. K. Olukoya laments, "Many of the challenges that we are facing are only remaining because they have not seen somebody to confront them with the kind of prayer that they need to be confronted with, and I am afraid a lot of men are faced with issues that their prayer altar is too weak to deal with."[390]

Weak standards lead to weak spirituality, weak prayers, and failure at the edge of breakthrough. Remember, personal change is not a mental activity, it involves adjusting how you live to be in alignment with where you know you need to be. In 1732 Thomas Fuller wrote, "They that worship God merely from fear would worship the devil, too, if he appear." Rather, from love and a depth of understanding of grace, we are compelled not by scarcity or fear, but by the abundance of receiving his unlimited favor. Why take such a gift and squander it away?

In an amazing statement, Isaiah says that God looked around the earth and "saw that there was no man, and wondered that there was no intercessor."[391] He was looking for someone who would pray "on earth, as it is in heaven," and live in the here and now from the perspective of eternity. He *wondered*, or questioned why no one stood in the gap for mankind.

John G. Lake demonstrated this powerfully when praying for a miracle and teaching others how to do so in their own lives and when praying for others. He taught that if people showed up *daily* for intense prayer for one month, they would see God's healing power within those 30 days. Some, he said, would need to do this for two months, and a small percent for three months, but as long as they continued to take believing action *every day*, their lives would be dramatically changed. The results seen in his ministry were astounding, with 100,000 documented cases of healing in 5 years.[392] Like Lake we each need to learn to be givers, ready to stand in the gap and pour our prayers and love into the lives of those around us.

Far too often, we experience the disappointment of selfish individuals. It is an odd experience to be in a checkout line that is growing full. You can feel the tension in the air as people become more and more impatient, wondering why the store only has one open aisle. Then finally, there is that moment of hope when the clerk uses the loudspeaker to call for assistance at the cash register.

In spite of their hopes, everyone suspects what will happen. The new register is opened and the clerk says, "I will take the person *next* in line." But it is a rare thing for that to happen. Almost without fail, other people will rush to that aisle and move ahead of the customers that have been waiting long before them, having no sense of responsibility to the rest of the people.

When I taught psychology at the university, often the most interesting discussions surrounded research into groups that were unaware they were being observed. One in particular stood out where a study was done by observing cars that ran stop lights and stop signs. The results were clear: the majority of infractions were committed by people driving expensive cars. The same was found on the highway in incidents involving tailgating, speeding, and dangerous lane changes. Unfortunately, entitlement breeds more entitlement. (Often, these selfsame entitled individuals are the ones who comment, "Doesn't it seem that people are getting ruder?").

In the process, we walk over one another, and we fail to notice or even care how our actions impact others. Yet, God wonders that there are not more people that take on the mind of Christ, and choose to stand in the gap for others instead of trampling over them in a mad rush to satisfy some selfish whim.

Andrew Murray wrote, "God rules the world and His church through the prayers of his people." When our hearts are small and our prayers are weak, we are missing the true calling placed before us. We must be clear on our confession that Christ is the life, and remove confessions of fear that contradict what we know to be true in our heart. The Psalmist tells us God "sent a man before them—Joseph, sold as a slave."[393] Heaven brings deliverance through men and women who cooperate with Jesus by stepping out in faith, just as Joseph was used to rescue his people from famine.

The Message paraphrase reminds us, "When you're in over your head, I'll be there with you. When you're in rough waters, you will not go down. When you're between a rock and a hard place, it won't be a dead end—Because I am God. I paid a huge price for you…That's how much you mean to me! That's how much I love you! So don't be afraid: I'm with you."[394]

When Sir John Templeton was asked for the secret to true wealth, he replied, "Gratitude." When we are grateful for who Jesus is, for what he is doing, and for what he has done, then we can move with more access to the throne of grace, with a spirit of expectation, far removed from the fears that hold so many back. As an unknown author wrote some time ago;

> Filled with a strange new hope they came,
> The blind, the leper, the sick, the lame.
> Frail of body and spent of soul …
> As many as touched Him were made whole.
>
> On every tongue was the Healer's name,
> Through all the country they spread His fame.
> But doubt clung tight to his wooden crutch
> Saying, "We must not expect too much."
>
> Down through the ages a promise came,
> Healing for sorrow and sin and shame,
> Help for the helpless and sight for the blind,
> Healing for the body and soul and mind.

The Christ we follow is still the same,
With blessings that all who will may claim.
But how often we miss Love's healing touch
By thinking, "We must not expect too much."

Isaiah says that God *wonders* that there are not more men and women who step out in faith and take hold of the abundant life he offers, with a joy and peace that will not rust or fade. What is the consequence of missing the mark? One is found in how the newest generation ranks in an unfortunate outcome.

It is estimated that Generation Z, those born since 1995, spend an average of three weeks out of the year on their phones, a record in and of itself. However, they are listed as number one in a category no one wants to make: they are the *loneliest* generation in America. There is wide debate on why this is so, but much of it stems from misguided parenting that has focused on achieving at the expense of building meaningful lives and relationships. All the technology and gadgets in the world serve only to distract for so long.

Real answers are only found in a faith that works, that leads to changed lives. We need to recognize that "faith is not the absence of doubt; it's the presence of belief."[395] What can we do differently? Appreciate the time we have been given, learn to redeem it day to day, live by a godly example, and seek to know more deeply the gift we have been given in Jesus so others can more clearly see the truth available for their lives. As an anonymous believer wrote, "Faith lives or dies not by what goes on in churches, but by what, as a result of the churches, goes on outside of them."

Recently, I listened as a speaker shared about going to the beach and seeing a sign at a lifeguard station that read, "If in doubt, *go!*" He related that the same sign needs to be on every church wall and on the heart of every believer as the world is in desperate need of people who will live out what they say they believe.

In the seventeenth century, William Penn wrote, "Time is what we want most, but what we use worst." Learn to focus on what matters most, give priority to eternal things, and learn to rest in the knowledge that Jesus' words are true. It *is* finished, so we can trust the work has been completed, and the tired wrestling match of seeking to be good enough has ended.

The oldest designation the church has for its self has always been "the Way."[396] The label is evidence of the understanding there is a right path, one meant to be followed.

It is said that a few years ago, a woman put an ad in the paper that simply stated, "Lost 50 lbs. Selling my fat clothes." She was bombarded with phone calls, but people were not interested in what she was selling; rather, they wanted to know what she had done to lose the weight.

When you live life with a different standard, people notice, and when they notice, they get curious. When authentic followers of the Way turned the world upside down in the first century, there was no denying their impact or their witness, and *everyone* noticed.

Much has been written about the words exchanged between Eve and the serpent. One interesting omission occurs when she tells the snake, "We may eat of the fruit of the trees of the garden."[397] In the original instruction, our parents were told, "Of every tree of the garden thou mayest *freely* eat,"[398] something Eve did not disclose. Eve had taken what was free and somehow put a price on it by making it sound off-limits. We are often tempted to put ourselves into the equation, but grace means that everything we receive is a gift of Christ, not something we earn.

Subsequently, the words given to Adam have been widely misunderstood. God was clear, if he were to eat from the forbidden tree, "in *the day* that thou eatest thereof thou shalt surely die"[399] Skeptics often point to this verse and question how Adam continued to live in spite of these prophetic words. The New Testament clarifies, "With the Lord a day is like a thousand years, and a thousand years are like a day."[400] We are told that Adam died at the age of 930,[401] well within "a day" from heaven's perspective. Even this was a sign of grace being unfolded.

After Adam, there was a man named Enoch who had a son named Methuselah. His name stood for, "when he dies it will come." He shared the earth for 600 years with his infamous grandson, Noah.[402] When he died, the floodwaters came, as his name implied. Here is another penetrating picture of grace, a living symbol to choose life over sin and selfishness. Judgment was promised in the form of a flood, but there were *centuries* given with a living breathing metaphor found in Methuselah, reminding people to turn their lives around.

Interestingly, it was during this same period that extremely long lifespans would come to an end. The promise after the flood was, "Their days will be a hundred and twenty years."[403] Remarkably, even science acknowledges that today, "the *maximum life potential*...has not changed and remains at 120 years."[404] Scripture is given to point us to true life, time and time again showing its accuracy in diagnosing the problems and solutions for our deepest wants and needs, if we but pay attention and listen.

In a fascinating piece of history, there is a beloved true story Billy Graham shared decades ago. Today, the tale has been updated into an urban legend involving a famous museum, contemporary politicians and well-known celebrities. The actual events took place well over a century ago, and the person of interest was Paul Morphy, a master chess player. Having dinner with some acquaintances, he found out the host had a picture hung on his wall of the devil playing chess with a young man, ready to declare checkmate and steal his soul. Gathering after the meal, Morphy studied the painting and told the other guests he could win the game for the lad. Exuberant, the host arranged a chessboard exactly as the pieces were positioned on the image. To everyone's delight, Morphy routed the devil and gained victory for the man in the painting.[405]

In the game of life, we are assured, "The reason the Son of God appeared was to destroy the devil's work."[406] You don't have to do this alone; surround yourself with people who pursue a higher level of expectation and service. Find others to join you on the path, and if need be hire a coach to help hold you accountable to your new standards. And lastly, be someone who doesn't just talk about it, but be someone who does the hard work of living your faith victoriously in this world gone mad.

NOTES

1. *Romeo Is Bleeding*. Dir. Peter Medak. Perf. Gary Oldman, Lena Olin, Annabella Sciorra, Juliette Lewis and Roy Scheider. Working Title Films, 1993. DVD.
2. Olukoya, D. (2004). *When God Declares a Man Non-existent*. 8(23), 5-6.
3. Wakely, Michael, *Can It Be True?* (Grand Rapids, MI: Kregel Publications, 2002), 207.
4. Roth, John D., *Choosing Against War* (Intercourse, PA: Good Books, 2002), 63.
5. Rome Reports. "African woman forgives criminals who murdered her family, visits one in prison." *YouTube*. YouTube, 14 June 2011. Web. 17 September 2018.
6. Benham, David and Benham, Jason, *Living among Lions*, (Nashville, TN: W Publishing Group, 2016), 80-81.
7. Hamilton, Adam, *Love to Stay* (Nashville, TN: Abingdon Press, 2013), 81.
8. Dalio, Ray, *Principles* (New York: NY, Simon & Schuster, 2017), 108.
9. 1 Corinthians 3:3
10. Robbins, Anthony, *Awaken the Giant Within* (New York, NY: Summit Books, 1992), 70.
11. Robbins, Anthony, *Unshakeable* (New York, NY: Simon & Schuster, 2017), 73.
12. Howard-Brown, Rodney and Williams, Paul L., *The Killing of Uncle Sam* (Tampa, FL: River Publishing, 2018), 25.
13. Ecclesiastes 5:10
14. Jeremiah 17:5
15. Cloud, David W. *Rock & Roll's War against God* (Port Huron, MI: Way of Life Literature, 2015), 80-83.

16 Bollinger, Ty, *Cancer – Step Outside the Box* (Infinity 510 Squared Partners, 2009), 37.

17 Proverbs 9:8

18 Lakhiani, Vishen, *The Code of the Extraordinary Mind* (New York, NY: Rodale, 2016), 53.

19 Morehouse, David, *Remote Viewing* (Boulder, CO: Sounds True, Inc., 2008), 6.

20 Robison, Eric, *Bending God* (Portland, OR: Higher Balance Publishing, 2007), 38.

21 Andreas, Joel, *Addicted to War* (Oakland, CA: AK Press, 2002), 40.

22 John 18:37

23 Jackson, Bill, *The Quest for the Radical Middle* (Cape Town, South Africa: Vineyard International Publishing, 1999), 292.

24 Matthew 3:2

25 McClendon, Joseph, *Get Happy Now* (Lake Dallas, TX: Success Books, 2011), 1.

26 Morrow, Alvin, *Breaking the Curse of Willie Lynch* (St. Louis, MO: Rising Sun Publications, 2003), 32.

27 Klein, Grady, *Psychology* (New York, NY: W. W. Norton & Company, 2018), 143.

28 Arntz, William and Chasse, Betsy and Vicente, Mark, *What the Bleep Do We Know?* (Deerfield Beach, FL: Health Communications, Inc., 2005), 147.

29 Comings, David E., *Did Man Create God?* (Duart, CA: Hope Press, 2008), 180.

30 Bragg, Patricia, *Super Power Breathing* (Santa Barbara, CA: Health Science, 2005), 28.

31 Roberts, Ted, *Pure Desire* (Ventura, CA: Regal, 1999), 173.

32 Vaden, Rory, *Take the Stairs* (New York, NY: TarcherPerigee, 2012), 31-32.

33 Brooks, Jeffrey M., *Rhinoceros Zen* (Bronx, NY: Fighting Arts, 2005), 63.

34 Lakhiani, 65.

35 Williams, Montel, *Living Well Emotionally* (New York, NY: New American Library, 2009), 67.

36 Ashley, Kurek, *How Would Love Respond* (Dallas, TX: Benbella Books, Inc., 2008), 309-310.

37 Long, Gerard, *The Breakthrough* (Deerfield, IL: Alpha North America, 2010), 70.

38 Malkmus, George H., *Why Christians Get Sick* (Shippensburg, PA: Treasure House, 2005), 28.

39 Jeffrey, Grant R., *The Signature of God* (Colorado Springs, CO: Waterbrook Press, 2010), 122.

40 Psalm 139:14

41 King, Richard and King, Susan, *Confusion* (Oconto, WI: Gigatt Books, 2012), 154.

42 Frizzell, Gregory, *Powerful Prayer for Every Family* (Oklahoma City, OK: Gregory R. Frizzell: 2010), 1.

43 Dowgiewicz, Mike and Sue, *Demolishing Strongholds* (Colorado Springs, CO: Restoration Ministries, 1995), 13.

44 Arush, Shalom, *The Garden of Peace* (Jerusalem, Israel: Chut Shel Chassed Institutions, 2008), 37.

45 Ibid. 159.

46 Genesis 2:24

47 Deida, David, *The Way of the Superior Man* (Boulder, CO: Sounds True, Inc., 2004), 53.

48 Gray, John, *Conscious Men* (Nevada City, CA: Self X Press, 2015), 67.

49 Marshall, Tom, *Free Indeed!* (Chichester, England: Sovereign World, 1983), 46.

50 1 Corinthians 7:4

51 Ephesians 5:25

52 Madanes, Cloe, *Relationship Breakthrough* (New York, NY: Rodale, 2009), 5.

53 Trimm, Cindy, *Commanding Your Morning* (Lake Mary, FL: Charisma House, 2007), 34.

54 Bragg, Patricia, *The Miracle of Fasting* (Santa Barbara, CA: Health Science, 2004), 132.

55 Cannon and Cannon, M.C. and Wilkinson, W., *Awakening from the American Dream* (San Diego, CA: Waterfront Digital Press, 2014), 1.

56 Colbert, Don, *Deadly Emotions* (Nashville, TN: Thomas Nelson, 2006), 13.

57 Epstein, Mark, *Open to Desire* (New York, NY: Gotham Books, 2005), 87.

58 Burwick, Ray, *The Menace Within* (Birmingham, AL: Ray Burwick, 1985), 44.

59 1 Timothy 6:19.

60 Williams, 57.

61 Duncan, Wendy J. *I Can't Hear God Anymore* (Rowlet, TX: VM Life Resources, LLC, 2006), 99.

62 Psalm 118.

63 Moore, Robert and Gillette, Douglas *King, Warrior, Magician, Lover* (New York, NY: Harper San Francisco, 1990(, 53.

64 Pendergrast, Mark, *Victims of Memory* (Hinesburg, VT: Upper Access Books, 1995), 133.

65 Morrow, 32.

66 Fitzpatrick, Owen, *Conversations with Richard Bandler* (Deerfield Beach, FL: Health Communications, Inc., 2009), 68.

67 Wilson, Colin, *Mysteries* (New York, NY: G. P. Putnam's Sons, 1978), 34.

68 Philippians 3:14

69 1 Peter 2:9

70 Fuhrman, John, *Reject Me – I Love it!* (Hummelstown, PA: Success Publishers, 1997), 27.

71 Nissen, Henri, *The God of Miracles* (Copenhagen, NV: Scandinavia Publishing House, 2003), 97-98.

72 Tepperwein, Kurt, *Master Secrets of Hypnosis and Self-Hypnosis* (New York, NY: Instant Improvement, Inc., 1991), 42-43.

73 Andry, Doran J. and McClendon III, Joseph, *The Burning Desire* (no city: Ignite Global Communication, 2005), 103.

74 Blunt, David M., *The Power of Expectation* (Mechanicsburg, PA: Church on the Rock, 1998), 17.

75 Graziosi, Dean, *Millionaire Success Habits* (Phoenix, AZ, Growth Publishing, 2017), 120-121.

76 Royle, Jonathan, *Confessions of a Hypnotist* (Bloomington, IN: Xlibris, 2006), 44.

77 Tereshchenko, Yuri, *Invoke a Blessing on Yourself* (Ft. Worth, TX: Yuri I. Tereshchenko, 2010), 40.

78 Pritchett, Price, *Hard Optimism* (New York, NY: McGraw-Hill), 11.

79 Ibid. 58.
80 Ragnar, Peter, *Success Seekers Guide to the Opulent Reality* (Ashville, NC: Roaring Lion Publishing Corp, 2007), 76.
81 Hall, Michael L. and Belnap, Barbara P., *The Sourcebook of Magic* (Carmarthen, Wales: Crown House Publishing Limited, 2000), 38.
82 Robbins, Anthony, *Notes From a Friend* (New York, NY: Fireside, 1995), 63.
83 Klein, 100.
84 Raley, Jim, *Hell's Spells* (Lake Mary, FL: Charisma House, 2012), 67.
85 Joshua 14:12
86 Blanchard, John, *Does God Believe in Atheists?* (Auburn, MA: Evangelical Press, 2000), 556-557.
87 Used by permission.
88 Deuteronomy 33:27
89 2 Corinthians 1:20 (TSNT)
90 Avanzini, John, *Powerful Principles of Release* (Tulsa, OK: Harrison House, 1989), 23.
91 Mark 5:34, Luke 17:19
92 Luke 18:8
93 Mann, Donald C., *Battle Prayer for Divine Healing* (Greenwell Springs, LA: McDougal & Associates, 2011), 102.
94 Robbins, Anthony, *Unshakeable* (New York, NY: Simon & Schuster, 2017), 167.
95 Sgarbi, Vittorio, *In the Name of the Son* (New York, NY: Rizzoli International Publications, Inc., 2014), 1.
96 Ibid. 4.
97 Ibid. 2.
98 Romans 8:17
99 James 2:19
100 Gonzalez, Alain, *Bulk Up Fast* (no city: Human Evolution Publishing, 2017), XVI.
101 Ferris, Tim, *Tools of Titans* (New York, NY: Houghton Mifflin Harcourt Publishing Company, 2017), 149.

102 Bandler, Richard, *Get the Life You Want* (Deerfield Beach, FL: Health Communications, Inc., 2008), xxiv.

103 Vaknin, Shlomo, *The Big Book of NLP Techniques,* (Lexington, KY: Shlomo Vaknin, 2008), 75.

104 Genesis 16:8

105 Cannon, M.C. and Wilkinson, 11-12.

106 Albion, Mark, *Making a Life, Making a Living* (Boston, MA: Business Plus, 2000), 33.

107 Epstein, 62.

108 Ponder, Cathering, *The Millionaires of Genesis* (Marina del Rey, CA: DeVorss & Company, 1987), 6.

109 John 15:11, King James Version

110 Deida, 40.

111 Thurmon, Dan, *Success in Action* (Atlanta, GA: Action Press, 2005), 115.

112 Jakes, T.D., *Destiny* (New York, NY: Hachette Book Group, 2015), 89.

113 Maldonado, Guillermo, *How to Walk in the Supernatural Power of God* (New Kensington, PA: Whitaker House), 87.

114 Kunneman, Hank, *Barrier Breakers* (Shippensburg, PA: Destiny Image Publishers, Inc., 2011), 78.

115 Arntz, William and Chasse, Betsy and Vicente, Mark, 102-103.

116 Canfield, Jack, *The Success Principles* (New York, NY: William Morrow, 2005), 43.

117 Romans 12:2.

118 Vest, Freddy, *The Day I Died* (Lake Mary, FL: Charisma House, 2014), 150.

119 Ashley, 80-81.

120 Pendergrast, 76.

121 DeArteaga, William, *Quenching the Spirit* (Lake Mary, FL: Charisma House, 1996), 91.

122 Griggs, Richard A. *Psychology* (New York, NY: Worth Publishers, 2014), 95.

123 Matthew 5:47

124 Bandler, Richard and La Valle John, *Persuasion Engineering* (Capitola, CA: Meta Publications, Inc., 1996), 43.

125 http://www.nathanielbranden.com/sentence-completion-i

126 Used by permission.
127 James 2:18.
128 Kraybill, Donald B. and Nolt, Steven M. and Weaver-Zercher, David L., *Amish Grace* (San Francisco, CA: John Wiley & Sons, 2007), 72.
129 I Met the Master (author unknown)
130 Hybels, Bill, *Just Walk across the Room* (Grand Rapids, MI: Zondervan, 2006), 19.
131 Isaiah 50:8 (Emphasis added)
132 John 11:33, 38, King James Version
133 Isaiah 14:16, King James Version
134 Harrison, 91.
135 Alcorn, Randy, *Money, Possessions and Eternity* (Wheaton, IL: Tyndale Publishers, Inc., 2003), 115.
136 Copeland, Kenneth, *The Blessing of the Lord* (Fort Worth, TX: Kenneth Copeland Publications, 2011), 187.
137 Vaknin, 481.
138 Cho, David Yonggi, *4th-Dimensional Living in a 3-Dimensional* World (Alachua, FL: Bridge-Logos, 2008), 131.
139 Moore and Gillette, 61.
140 Bickle, Mike, *Growing in Prayer* (Lake Mary, FL: Charisma Media/Charisma House Book Group, 2014), 39.
141 Madanes, Cloe, *Strategic Family Therapy* (San Francisco, CA: Jossey-Bass Publishers, 1981), 35-36.
142 Jude 1:12 (TSNT)
143 2 Thessalonians 2:4, King James Version (Emphasis added)
144 Arush, 138.
145 Duin, Julia, *Quitting Church* (Grand Rapids, MI: Baker Books, 2008), 123.
146 John 15:11
147 1 Peter 1:8
148 Ross, Allen P., *Holiness to the Lord* (Grand Rapids, MI: Baker Academic, 2002), 321.
149 Isaiah 1:18

150 Footnote *Yoma 39b, Babylonian Talmud*, Soncino Press Edition.

151 John 10:30

152 DeFazio, James J., *The Tithe* (Matinland, FL: Xulon Press, 2007), 207.

153 Bryan, David, *Christ is All* (New Providence, NJ: New Providence Publishers, 2005), 21.

154 Hebrews 9:24

155 Volf, Miroslav, *Free of Charge* (Grand Rapids, MI: Zondervan, 2006), 55.

156 John 5:5-6

157 John 5:7

158 Bevere, John, *Drawing Near* (Nashville, TN: Thomas Nelson, 2004), 11.

159 Lozoff, 20.

160 Romans 6:4 (Emphasis added)

161 Tarcher, Jeremy P. (Ed.), *The Prosperity Bible* (New York, NY: Penguin Group, 2006), 862.

162 Hebrews 1:2 (Emphasis added)

163 Acts 24:14

164 Revelation 13:18

165 Acts 1:3

166 Moore, Johnnie, *Defying Isis* (Nashville, TN: W Publishing Group, 2015), 73. (emphasis added)

167 Phipps, Wintley, *The Power of a Dream* (Grand Rapids, MI: Zondervan Publishing House, 1994), 84.

168 1 Thessalonians 4:14

169 Liardon, Roberts, *John G. Lake: The Complete Collection of His Life Teachings* (Tulsa, OK: Albury Publishing, 1999), 124.

170 Floyd, Ronnie, *Life on Fire* (Nashville, TN: W Publishing Group, 2000), 34.

171 Armstrong, Robb, *Fearless* (White Plains, NY: Reader's Digest Trade Publishing, 2016), 112.

172 2 Corinthians 3:17

173 Baxter, J. Sidlow, *For God So Loved* (Grand Rapids, MI: Kregel Classics, 1995), 143-144.

174 Yoder, Barbara J., *Taking on Goliath* (Lake Mary, FL: Charisma House, 2009), 160.

175 Revelation 3:20

176 2 Corinthians 12:7

177 Hebrews 4:2

178 Isaiah 63:9

179 Galatians 6:2

180 Daniel 9:20, King James Version (Emphasis added)

181 Daniel 9:23, King James Version (Emphasis added)

182 Philippians 4:6

183 Trousdale, Jerry, *Miraculous Movements* (Nashville, TN: Thomas Nelson, 2012), 53.

184 Harrison, Nick, *Magnificent Prayer* (Grand Rapids, MI: Zondervan, 2001), 101.

185 Cerullo, Morris, *Lord, Teach us to Pray* (San Diego, CA: Morris Cerullo World Evangelism, 2005), 97.

186 Matthew 18:19, King James Version (Emphasis added)

187 Brandt, Robert L. and Bicket, Zenas J. *The Spirit Helps us Pray* (Springfield, MO: Gospel House Publishing, 1993), 47.

188 Rutland, Mark, *21 Seconds to Change Your World* (Bloomington, MN: Bethany House Publications, 2016), 19.

189 Marion, Jim, *Putting on the Mind of Christ* (Charlottesville VA: Hampton Roads Publishing Company, Inc., 2000), 159.

190 2 Corinthians 4:4

191 Perry, Philippa, *Couch Fiction* (New York, NY: Palgrave MacMillan, 2010), 149.

192 Psalm 121:2

193 *Road House*. Dir. Rowdy Herrington. Perf. Patrick Swayze, Kelly Lynch, Sam Elliott, and Ben Gazzara. United Artists, 1989. DVD.

194 Kübler-Ross, Elisabeth. *Going Home*. Monroe Products, 2004.

195 Jeffreys, Michael, *Success Secrets of the Motivational Superstars* (Rocklin, CA: Prima Publishing, 1996.), 35.

196 Walker, Daniel, *God in a Brothel* (Downers Grove, IL: InterVarsity Press, 2011), 53.

197 Luke 19:13
198 Matthew 6:4
199 1 Samuel 17:29, King James Version
200 Fuhrman, 49.
201 Mac, Toby, *City on Our Knees* (Minneapolis, MN: Bethany House, 2010), 39.
202 Ademola, Toye, *Seven Secrets of Bible Made Millionaires* (no city, AZ: Selah Publishing Group, LLC, 2007), 22.
203 Rutland, Mark, *21 Seconds to Change Your World* (Minneapolis, MN: Bethany House Publishers, 2019), 10.
204 Ephesians 5:25
205 Ecclesiastes 5:6
206 Ephesians 1:18
207 Sturm, Lacey, *The Reason* (Grand Rapids, MI: Baker Books, 2014), 169.
208 Hedges, Chris, *What Every Person Should Know About War* (New York, NY: Free Press, 2003), 33-34.
209 Roberts, 65.
210 Perloff, James, *Tornado in a Junkyard* (Arlington, MA: Refuge Books, 1999), 221.
211 Johnson, Joey, *God is Greater Than...Family Mess* (Enumclaw, WA: WinePress Publishing, 2003), 18.
212 John 18:38
213 Zechariah 4:10
214 Houston, Brian, *Live Love Lead* (New York, NY: FaithWords, 2015), 58.
215 Acts 5:41
216 Arush, 155-156.
217 Dalio, 77.
218 Fuhrman, 54.
219 2 Kings 7:3
220 2 Kings 7:10, 16
221 Buzzard, Sir Anthony F., *The One God, the Father, One Man Messiah Translation* (Restoration Fellowship: 2014), 56.

222 Grady, William P., *How Satan Turned America Against God* (Knoxville, TN: Grady Publications Inc., 2005), 91-94.

223 Lucado, Max, *Cure for the Common Life* (Nashville, TN: W Publishing Group, 2007), 15.

224 Murphey, Cecil, *Prayerobics* (Waco, TX: Word Books, 1979), 38.

225 Gray, John, *Beyond Mars and Venus* (Dallas, TX: BeBella Books, Inc., 2017), 32.

226 Beeson, Ray, *Signed in His Blood* (Lake Mary, FL: Charisma House, 2014), 117-118.

227 Gire, Ken, *Between Heaven and Earth* (New York, NY: HarperCollins, 1997), 71.

228 Mark 16:7 (Emphasis added)

229 Bright, Bill, *God* (Orlando, FL: New Life Publications, 1999), 80.

230 Newberg, Andrew and Waldman, Mark Robert, *Why We Believe What We Believe* (New York, NY: Free Press, 2006), 4.

231 Hughes, Kent, *Disciplines of a Godly Man* (Wheaton, IL: Crossway Books, 2001), 25.

232 Romans 11:32 (Emphasis added)

233 Butt, Howard Jr., *Who Can You Trust?* (WaterBrook Press: Colorado Springs, 2004), 57-59.

234 Matthew 11:28-30

235 Ephesians 3:18

236 Elliot, Elisabeth, *Through Gates of Splendor* (New York, NY: Harper and Brothers, 1957), 18.

237 Foxe, John and The Voice of the Martyrs, *Foxe* (Alachua, FL: Bridge-Logos, 2007), 241.

238 Garlow, James L., *God and His People* (New York, NY: Victor, 2004), 26.

239 Matthew 7:7

240 Meals Ready-to-Eat

241 1 Samuel 17:40

242 2 Samuel 21:22

243 Ellis, Anthony, *Gaining Mass* (New York, NY: Cutting Edge Publishing, Inc., 2002), 5.

244 Poulin, Kaelin Tuell, *Big Fat Lies* (Pasadena, CA: Best Seller Publishing, 2017), 80.
245 Canfield, Jack, *The Success Principles* (New York, NY: William Morrow, 2004), 178.
246 Hughes, 13.
247 Levine, Stuart R. *...Cut to the Chase* (New York, NY: Doubleday, 2006), 1.
248 Matthew 11:21
249 Matthew 8:23
250 Osteen, Dodie, *If My Heart Could Talk* (New York, NY: FaithWords, 2016), 123.
251 Anderson, Clinton, *Lessons Well Learned* (North Pomfret, VT: Trafalgar Square Books, 2009), 100.
252 Maxwell, John, *Failing Forward* (Nashville, TN: Thomas Nelson, 2000), 47-48.
253 Morehouse, 73.
254 Bandler, Richard, *Time for a Change* (Capitola, CA: Meta Publications, Inc., 1993), 86-87.
255 Matthew 6:2
256 Moseley, Ron, *Yeshua* (Baltimore, MD: Lederer Books, 1996), 28.
257 Matthew 15:12
258 Matthew 22:15-21
259 Mac, 116.
260 Hendrickson, Mark, *Supernatural Provision* (Shippensburg, PA: Destiny Image Publishers, Inc., 2011), 51.
261 Chilton, David, *The Days of Vengeance* (Tyler, TX: Dominion Press, 1987), 553.
262 Crowder, John, *The New Mystics* (Shippensburg, PA: Destiny Image Publishers, Inc., 2006), 117.
263 Wilkins, Michael, *Matthew: From Biblical Text to Contemporary Life, NIV Application Commentary Series* (Grand Rapids, MI: Zondervan, 2004), 739.
264 Matthew 27:32-33
265 1 Corinthians 15:45-46
266 Forde, Gerhard O., *On Being a Theologian of the Cross* (Grand Rapids, MI: William B. Eerdman's Publishing Group, 1997), 3.
267 Lucado, Max, *Glory Days* (Nashville, TN: Thomas Nelson, 2015), 179.

268 Blasier, Clarence L. *The Prayer for Abundant Favor* (North Canton, OH: Matthew Publishing Company, 2002), 81.

269 Wiens, Gary, *Bridal Intercession* (Greenwood, MO: Oasis House, 2001), 111.

270 Brown, Michael H. *Prayer of the Warrior* (Milford, OH: Faith Publishing Company, 1993), 110.

271 Illona, Monique, *A Dual Path* (Marblehead, MA: Dual Path Press, 2014), 22.

272 Bernis, Jonathan, *Confessing the Hebrew Scriptures* (Phoenix, AZ: JVMI Publishing, 2011), 2.

273 Jeffrey, 37.

274 Hebrews 4:12

275 Buckingham, Jamie, *Summer of Miracles* (Lake Mary, FL: Creation House, 1991), 73.

276 Thurmon, 84.

277 Alcorn, Randy, *Heaven* (Carol Stream, IL: Tyndale House Publishers, 2007), xxii.

278 Ephesians 2:20 (Emphasis added)

279 2 Corinthians 11:24-25, New King James Version

280 Renner, Rick, *Sparkling Gems From the Greek* (Tulsa, OK: Teach All Nations, 2003), 793.

281 Galatians 6:17

282 Job 19:25

283 Maxwell, John, *Failing Forward* (Nashville, TN: Thomas Nelson Inc., 2000), 43.

284 Romans 10:15

285 1 Corinthians 6:17

286 Volkman, Bill (Ed.), *Infinite Supply* (Glen Ellyn, IL: Union Life Ministries, 1980) 19.

287 Foxe, John and The Voice of the Martyrs, *Foxe* (Alachua, FL: Bridge-Logos, 2007), 235.

288 Gray, John, *Conscious Men*, 15.

289 Hamilton, 137.

290 Twyman, James F., *The Moses Code* (New York, NY: Hay House, Inc., 2008), 114

291 Galatians 6:7
292 Lozoff, Bo, We're All Doing Time (Dunham, NC: Human Kindness Foundation, 1985), 9.
293 Ibid, 11.
294 Avanzini, 40.
295 Williamson, Desi, *Get Off Your Assets* (Dubuque, IO: Kendall/Hunt Publishing Company, 1996), 144.
296 John 14:1-3
297 Wiens, 91-92.
298 Duin, Julia, *Quitting Church* (Grand Rapids, MI: Baker Books, 2008), 114.
299 Nouwen, Henri J.M., *The Return of the Prodigal Son* (New York, NY: Image Books/Doubleday Publishing Group, 1994), 82.
300 Card, Michael, *A Sacred Sorrow* (Colorado Springs, CO: NavPress, 2005), 29.
301 Smith, Douglas, C., *Being a Wounded Healer* (Madison, WI: Psycho-Spiritual Publications, 1999), 48.
302 Ephesians 4:29
303 Anderson, Neil T. and Mylander, Charles, *Setting Your Church Free* (Ventura, CA: Gospel Light Publications, 1999), 214.
304 Galatians 2:20
305 Matthew 26:30 (Emphasis added)
306 Psalm 118:1
307 Psalm 118:6
308 Psalm 118:17
309 Luke 22:53
310 Psalm 118:29
311 Sometimes attributed to James Allen Francis
312 Anthony, Ole, *Crossfire* (Plainfield, NJ: Logos International, 1976), 210. Used by permission.
313 Amos 3:8
314 Matthew 1:21
315 Genesis 27:36
316 Genesis 32:28

317 Genesis 17:5
318 Numbers 13:16
319 Believed to be pronounced *Yahweh*.
320 Ross, Allen P. *Holiness to the Lord* (Grand Rapids, MI: Baker Academic, 2002), 446.
321 Revelation 2:17
322 John 14:22
323 Fuhrman, 25.
324 Oliver, Tom, *Nothing is Impossible* (New York, NY: McGraw-Hill Education, 2014), 31.
325 Royle, 107.
326 Nissen, Henri, *The God of Miracles* (Copenhagen, NV: Scandinavia Publishing House, 2003), 157.
327 Stone, Perry, *The Meal that Heals* (Lake Mary, FL: Charisma House, 2008), 3.
328 John 10:10
329 Luke 9:23
330 Volkman, Bill (Ed.), *Infinite Supply* (Glen Ellyn, IL: Union Life Ministries, 1980) 14.
331 Colossians 1:27
332 Duncan, 183.
333 Philippians 3:8
334 Lerner, Michael, *Spirit Matters* (Newburyport, MA: Hampton Roads Publishing, 2002), 106.
335 Jacobs, Cindy, *Possessing the Gates of the Enemy* (Grand Rapids, MI: Baker Book House Company, 1991), 57.
336 North, Gary, *Unholy Spirits* (Ft. Worth, TX: Dominion Press, 1986), 8-9.
337 Brown, 79.
338 Godwin, Jeff, *Dancing With Demons* (Chino, CA: Chick Publications, 1988), 196-198.
339 Psalm 61:2
340 Philippians 4:13, King James Version

341 Maxwell, John, *Talent is Never Enough* (Nashville, TN: Thomas Nelson, 2007), 211.

342 Luke 17:20-21

343 Litzman, Warren, *Jesus Lost in the Church* (Shippensburg, PA: Treasure House, 1993), 39.

344 Colossians 1:27 (Emphasis added)

345 Romans 6:1

346 Romans 6:2

347 Zimmerman, Lynne, *Heal Yourself* (North Branch, MN: Sunrise River Press, 2011), 51-52.

348 Hall, Michael L. and Belnap, Barbara P., 25.

349 Stone, Dave, *Refining Your Style* (Loveland, CO: Group Publishing, 2004), 191.

350 Nicholi, Armand M. Jr., *The Question of God* (New York, NY: Free Press, 2003), 61.

351 Chan, Francis, *Crazy Love* (Colorado Springs, CO: David C. Cook, 2008), 27.

352 Boy, Don, *Evolution: Fact or Fiction* (Largo, FL: Freedom Publications, 1994), 123.

353 Stanley, Colin, *Colin Wilson's 'Occult Trilogy* (Nottingham, UK: Axis Mundi Books, 2012), 13.

354 Colossians 1:27

355 Luke 15:17

356 Luke 15:20

357 1 Samuel 21:4

358 John 6:35

359 1 Samuel 21:9 (Emphasis added)

360 1 Samuel 21:11

361 Robbins, *Unshakeable*, 182.

362 Auch, Ron, *Prayer can Change Your Marriage* (Green Forest, AR: New Leaf Press, 1992), 17.

363 Galli, Mark, *A Great and Terrible Love* (Grand Rapids, MI: Baker Books, 2009), 61-62.

364 Psalm 139:8

365 Fuhrman, 18.
366 Hebrews 13:5
367 Blanchard, 66-67.
368 Colson, Charles, *God and Government* (Zondervan, 2007), 57-60.
369 Jeffreys, 22.
370 Pelletier, Ray, *Permission to Win* (Winchester, VA: OakHill Press, 1996), 14.
371 Olayeri, Tella, *Hidden Treasures Exposed* (Isua Akoko, Ondo State: God's Link Ventures, 2009), 197.
372 Monahan, Brian, *The Faith* (New York, NY: Image, 2003), 85.
373 John 19:5
374 Moseley, 122-123.
375 Luke 17:11-19
376 Matthew 9:27-34
377 Matthew 9:33
378 John 9:32
379 John 11:39
380 John 11:53
381 Haggai 2:7
382 Sifakis, Carl (Ed.), *The Big Book of Hoaxes* (New York, NY: Paradox Press, 1996), 100-101.
383 Romans 7:15
384 Deuteronomy 23:23, Christian Standard Bible
385 Haley, Jay, *Uncommon Therapy* (New York, NY: W. W. Norton and Company, Inc., 1986), 26.
386 Hebrews 12:14, King James Version
387 Hebrews 12:16
388 Alcorn, Randy, *Money, Possessions and Eternity*, 122.
389 Colossians 1:27
390 Olukoya, D. K., *Prayer Compass* (Ikeja, Lagos: The Battle Cry Christian Ministries, 2017), 203.
391 Isaiah 59:16

392 Mann, 126.

393 Psalm 105:17

394 Isaiah 43:2-7

395 Moraine, Jack, *Healing Ministry* (Choctaw, OK: HGM Publishing, 2010), 62.

396 Acts 9:2

397 Genesis 3:2, King James Version

398 Genesis 2:16, King James Version (Emphasis added)

399 Genesis 2:17, King James Version (Emphasis added)

400 2 Peter 3:8

401 Genesis 5:5

402 Genesis 7:11

403 Genesis 6:3

404 Shermer, Michael, *Heavens on Earth* (New York, NY: Henry Holt and Company, 2018), 256.

405 "The 'One More Move' Story of Paul Morphy and the Moritz Retzsch Painting", https://www.one-more-move-chess-art.com/One-More-Move.html, (September 21, 2018)

406 1 John 3:8

www.ingramcontent.com/pod-product-compliance
Lightning Source LLC
Chambersburg PA
CBHW070143100426
42743CB00013B/2812